ANDREW DEMPSTER has almost 50 years' experience of walking, scrambling and backpacking in the Scottish Highlands and Islands. He has climbed all the Munros three times and is well on his way to completion of a fourth round. He has also completed all the Corbetts and Grahams and wrote the first guidebook to the Grahams. He has also trekked and climbed extensively in such varied locations as the Alps, the Pyrenees, the Himalayas, the USA, Africa, Iceland, Greenland and Patagonia. The Highlands of Scotland are his first love, however. He is a retired mathematics teacher, currently living in rural Perthshire with his wife Heather. He has a son, Ruaraidh and a stepdaughter, Laura.

By the same author:

Classic Mountain Scrambles in Scotland (Mainstream, 1992; Luath, 2016)
The Munro Phenomenon (Mainstream, 1995)
The Grahams: A Guide to Scotland's 2,000ft Peaks (Mainstream, 1997)
Skye 360: Walking the Coastline (Luath, 2003)
100 Classic Coastal Walks in Scotland (Mainstream, 2011)
The Hughs Vol 1 – The Mainland: Scotland's Best Wee Hills under 2,000 ft
(Luath, 2015)
Classic Mountain Scrambles in Scotland (Luath reprint, 2016)
The Munros: A History (Luath, 2021)

The Hughs

Vol. 2: The Islands

Scotland's Best Wee Hills under 2,000ft

ANDREW DEMPSTER

Luath Press Limited

EDINBURGH

www.luath.co.uk

First published 2026

ISBN: 978-1-91214-734-2

The paper used in this book is recyclable. It is made from
low-chlorine pulps produced in a low-energy, low-emission
manner from renewable forests.

Printed and bound by
Hobbs the Printers Ltd., Totton

Typeset in Sabon by
Main Point Books, Edinburgh

Contents

Introduction 9
Key to Using this Guide 18

PART I: THE SOUTHERN ISLES AND INNER HEBRIDES (50 HUGHS)

THE FIRTH OF CLYDE TO FIRTH OF LORN – HUGHS MAP 21

The Firth of Clyde and Kintyre

1	The Cairn (Ailsa Craig)	22
2	Mullach Mòr (Holy Island)	25
3	Meall nan Damh (Arran)	28
4	Davaar summit (Davaar)	31

Islay, Jura and surrounding islands

5, 6	Glas Bheinn and Beinn Bheigier (Islay)	33
7	Sgòrr nam Faoileann (Islay)	36
8	Sgarbh Breac (Islay)	39
9	Glas Bheinn (Jura)	41
10, 11	Scrinadle and Corra Bheinn (Jura)	43
12	Carnan Eoin (Colonsay)	46
13	Cruach Scarba (Scarba)	49

MULL TO RUM – HUGHS MAP 53

Mull and surrounding islands

14, 15	Beinn na Sreine and Creach Bheinn (Mull)	54
16	Beinn a' Ghraig (Mull)	57
17	Beinn na Duatharach (Mull)	59
18	Speinne Mòr (Mull)	62
19	'S Àirde Beinn (Mull)	64
20	Dun I (Iona)	66
21	Beinn Chreagach (Ulva)	68

Tiree and the Small Isles

22	Beinn Ceann a' Mhara (Tiree)	70
23	An Sgùrr (Eigg)	73
24, 25	Bloodstone Hill and Orval (Rum)	76

SKYE AND RAASAY – HUGHS MAP   79

Skye and Raasay

26, 27	Beinn na Cro and Glas Bheinn Mhòr (Skye)	80
28	Sgùrr na Strì (Skye)	83
29	Ruadh Stac	88
30, 31	Beinn a' Bhraghad and An Cruachan (Skye)	90
32, 33	Preshal Beg and Preshal More (Skye)	93
34	Ben Tianavaig (Skye)	96
35, 36	Healabhal Mhòr and Healabhal Bheag (Skye)	98
37	Waterstein Head (Skye)	101
38	Biod an Athair (Skye)	103
39	Sithean Bhealaich Chumhaing (Skye)	105
40	Ben Dearg (Skye)	107
41	Sgùrr a Mhadaidh Ruaidh (Skye)	109
42, 43	Bioda Buidhe and Cleat (Skye)	111
44–46	Quiraing East Peak and Sron Vourlinn and Meall na Suiramach (Skye)	114
47, 48	Leac nan Fionn and Dun Mor (Skye)	117
49	Dùn Caan (Raasay)	121
50	Beinn na h-Iolaire (Raasay)	124

PART 2: THE NORTHERN ISLES AND OUTER HEBRIDES (50 HUGHS)

ORKNEY AND SHETLAND – HUGHS MAP   129

Orkney and Shetland

51, 52	Cuilags and Ward Hill (Hoy, Orkney)	130
53	Da Sneug (Foula, Shetland)	133

MINGULAY TO NORTH UIST – HUGHS MAP   139

Mingulay, Barra and Eriskay

54	Carnan (Mingulay)	140
55	Heabhal (Barra)	143
56	Beinn Tangabhal (Barra)	145
57	Beinn Sciathan (Eriskay)	147

South Uist, Benbecula and North Uist

58–60	Beinn Ruigh Choinnich and Triuirebheinn and Stulabhal (South Uist)	149
61, 62	Thacla (Hecla) and Beinn Choradail (South Uist)	152
63	Ruabhal (Benbecula)	155
64	Eabhal (Eaval) (North Uist)	157
65	Lì a Tuath (North Lee) (North Uist)	160

HARRIS/LEWIS AND SURROUNDING ISLANDS – HUGHS MAP   163

Harris

66	Roineabhal (South Harris)	165
67	Bleabhal (South Harris)	167
68	Ceapabhal (South Harris)	169
69	Beinn Dhubh (South Harris)	171
70, 71	Sgaoth Aird and Giolabhal Glas (North Harris)	173
72	Todun (North Harris)	176
73–75	Ceartabhal and Huiseabhal and Leosabhal (North Harris)	178
76, 77	Stulabhal and Liuthaid (North Harris)	181

The Shiant Islands

78   Mullach Buidhe   184

Lewis

79–81   Guaineamol and Muaitheabhal and Feiriosbhal (Pairc)   188
82, 83   Beinn Mhòr and Caiteseal (Pairc)   191
84   Gormol (Pairc)   197
85   Roineabhal   199
86, 87   Griomabhal and Laibheal a' Tuath (West Lewis)   202
88, 89   Mealaisbhal and Cracabhal (West Lewis)   204
90–93   Tamnasbhal and Teinneasabhal and Tathabhal and Tarain (West Lewis)   207
94, 95   Suaineabhal and Sron ri Gaoith (West Lewis)   210
96   Beinn Bhragair (North Lewis)   213

St Kilda

97–99   Oisebhal and Conachair and Mullach Bi (Hirta)   215
100   Mullach an Eilein (Boreray)   219

Index of Hill Names and Islands   222

INTRODUCTION

The author on Sgùrr na Strì (Skye)

Introducing Volume 2 of *The Hughs*

THIS BOOK IS the second of two volumes covering the Scottish hills known as the Hughs (Hills Under Graham Height in Scotland). Volume 1 dealt with the 100 mainland Hughs and Volume 2 covers the 100 island Hughs.

This introduction is not simply a rehash of the introduction to Volume 1 (although there is some repetition of salient points) but aims to inject more insight into the motivation and rationale for the Hughs list, particularly in relation to the special nature of island hills.

Birth of the Hughs

The Hughs were born from the essentially Scottish notion of classifying hills according to their height above sea level. The genesis of this idea was, of course, the class of hills identified and classified by Sir Hugh Munro over a century ago and universally known as the Munros – Scottish mountains over 3,000ft. Hot on the heels of this list came the Corbetts. This was a list compiled by Rooke J Corbett in the 1930s; all have a height between 2,500ft and 3,000ft. In addition, he implicitly included an extra criterion that each hill had a prominence of at least 500ft.

Some time later a subsequent Munroist, William M Docharty, went on to spend 14 years of his life classifying British mountain tops, resulting

in three brilliantly researched tomes covering all summits above 2,000ft and many below this height. Unfortunately, the limited number of copies made little impact on the hillwalking fraternity of the time. It actually took until the early 1990s before an official list of 2,000ft Scottish hills began to materialise.

Fiona Graham had tentatively begun to create such a list, later collaborating with Alan Dawson, who had already compiled a mega-list of all British summits having a prominence of 150m – regardless of height above sea level – known as the Marilyns. The name 'Marilyn' was allegedly a play on the name 'Marilyn Monroe', but the label has never invited universal appeal! The subset of these 1,500-plus hills, which are Scottish hills between 2,000ft and 2,500ft, came to be known as the Grahams.

That was essentially the end of the story; except that the subset of Marilyns consisting of all the Scottish hills below 2,000ft, did not have a specific name. Not only that, but this cumbersome sub 2,000ft list contained over 500 hills. The other three main lists of Munros, Corbetts and Grahams, in addition to having a distinct name, also contained a manageable number of hills; each list has between 200 and 300 hills. There was also no denying that the far larger 500 or so hills under 2,000ft, included a dross of relatively featureless, flat-topped high points, which, notwithstanding their prominence, were not inviting hills to climb. Conversely, despite the 150m drop criterion of the Marilyns, there are many fine hills in Scotland which refuse to conform to the sterile logic of relative height. Think of mainland hills such as Dumgoyne, Ben A'n and An Groban, or island hills such as Bloodstone Hill, Dun I and Sgùrr a Mhadaidh Ruaidh – none of these superb wee hills are Marilyns, but all are classic hills of Scotland, having a good dose of attitude.

The preceding arguments and ramblings had entered my head around the same time as I coined the acronym 'Hugh' to describe a Scottish hill below 2,000ft. I felt that there should be a separate category of Scottish hills below this height collectively known as the Hughs, but what criteria should be used for inclusion? After much wrestling and hand-wringing with relative height and absolute height, I was getting nowhere fast and decided to revert to subjective criteria. If a hill was worth climbing due to its character, prominence, panoramic summit views or whatever, then it should be included.

Of course, I was well aware that I was opening a can of worms with such nebulous, subjective notions and that I would be open to criticism from those whose favourite hill had not been included, and from others who wondered why on earth such and such a hill had been included. Despite these misgivings, I am amazed to say that for Volume 1 of *The Hughs*, I have so far not received a single criticism of my choice of hills. I am aware of course, that any critics out there may well be keeping a low profile, but I hope there are not too many!

Sgùrr a Mhadaidh Ruaidh (Skye)

Ben Tianavaig from Sithean Bhealaich Chumhaing (Skye)

The fact that there are exactly 200 Hughs, rightly requires some explanation. When I began to compile a tentative list of hills based on the subjective notions given above, I was genuinely astonished at what I found. Not only did the final count amount to just over 200 hills, but roughly half were mainland hills and half were island hills. So, already I had a list of hills roughly comparable in size to the Munros, Corbetts and Grahams lists, but these were 'hills of the heart' and hills with attitude. Trimming the list to a neat and round 200 hills was almost a compelling necessity and interestingly matched further forays into the hills to eliminate a few that did not 'make the grade'. Additional tidy subdivisions resulted in the final: 50 hills in South and East Scotland; 50 hills in North and West Scotland; 50 hills in the Southern Isles and Inner Hebrides and 50 hills in the Northern Isles and Outer Hebrides.

The Nature of Hughs

In the introduction to Volume 1 of *The Hughs*, I gave the defining characteristics or qualities of the Hughs to be prominence, position and panoramic views. These three qualities could be distilled into one word: attitude. Further ruminations on this have prompted me to include a fourth quality of 'presence'. The presence of a hill is more of a generalised term indicating its personality or character and is more subjective than the first three. It is perhaps worth repeating the observation of the iconic fell walker, AW Wainwright, when he said in his *Favourite Lakeland Mountains*:

The status of a mountain is not determined by any arbitrary level of altitude but by appearance. Rocks and ruggedness, roughness of terrain and a commanding presence are the essential qualifications.

The crucial phrase here is 'commanding presence'. This is a notion that all hill-walkers will recognise when gazing upon such hills as Arthur's Seat, Buachaille Etive Mòr, Suilven, Sgùrr na Strì, Stac Pollaidh, The Cobbler, Ben Tianavaig and Beinn Dhubh. The fact that these diverse examples consist of one Munro, one Corbett, two Grahams and four Hughs, ie a range of different altitudes, is irrelevant. It is not altitude which deter-mines character or presence, but attitude.

Not all Hughs will possess rocks and ruggedness or roughness of terrain, but still nevertheless have a commanding presence, perhaps due to their being the highest point for miles around, eg Speinne Mòr on the island of Mull; or for their distinctive topography, eg Dùn Caan on Raasay or An Sgùrr on Eigg.

Of course, there are many hills in Scotland, where the concept of 'com-manding presence' is a nebulous one. It is easy to list the ones which definitely do have this quality and also the ones which do not. However, in between, there is a sizeable proportion for which the term is a fuzzy concept and essen-tially subjective. Herein lies the person-al nature of the Hughs. The list is not defined by any foolproof, watertight rule of inclusion, such as for Corbetts

and Grahams. Just as the Munros are a list of hills over 3,000ft, with no firm criteria for inclusion ie they are a subjective list. Thus, the Hughs have more in common with the Munros than the Corbetts, Grahams, Donalds and indeed, Marilyns. The fact that Hugh Munro's first name coincides with this list is also somewhat appropriate!

Island Hills

Island hills possess a charm and romanticism which is hard to resist and sets them apart from their mainland cousins. The combination and juxtaposition of mountain, sea and sky so notably manifest on islands such as Arran, Jura, Mull, Rum and Skye can be as addictive and headily intoxicating as any malt whisky, capturing and enrapturing, often for life.

It is perhaps surprising that less than 50 of the hills in the 700 or so list of Munros, Corbetts and Grahams, are found on islands. In fact, the bulk of these hills are on the five islands mentioned above, with a further small sprinkling on Harris and South Uist. Yet Scotland contains literally hundreds of islands, many having smaller hills with character often exceeding that of many a Munro, Corbett or Graham. This is where the Hughs really come into their own, and perhaps nowhere better than the Outer Hebrides, which contain nearly half the hills in this book.

The Outer Hebrides have only one

Beinn Dhubh from Luskentyre (Harris)

Corbett and four Grahams (see end of introduction) comprising just a tiny sample of the host of smaller hills on offer. By far, the bulk of mountainous country in the Outer Isles consists of hills under 2,000ft. The rocky topography of these islands ensures that a sizeable majority of these hills have immense character and are therefore suitable contenders for Hugh status.

Outwith the Outer Hebrides, many of the remaining 50 Hughs are on the five large islands mentioned previously. Another large island – Islay – contains 4 Hughs, but no hills above 2,000ft. A significant proportion of Hughs, and indeed, some of the finest, are on small islands, some with no permanent population. These isolated outposts stretch to all points of the compass and include such diverse islets as Ailsa Craig, Scarba, Ulva, Mingulay, the Shiants, Foula and the St Kilda isles. Just reaching some of these islands is an expedition in itself, making the challenge of the island Hughs more than a mere walking/climbing quest.

Islands, Rocks and Stacks

When is an island not an island? This whimsical question has a deeper meaning, relevant to this book. Some sources dispute the status of Skye as an island, owing to its bridge connection to the mainland. My own view is that it is still surrounded by water, so it is still an island. I would also argue that

Eriskay in the Outer Hebrides is still an island, despite a causeway connection to South Uist.

However, the main thrust of this part of the introduction concerns rocks and stacks and I need to justify my exclusion of these in this book.

A handful of dedicated enthusiasts have now completed Alan Dawson's list of over 1,500 Marilyns, finishing on what are deemed to be the 'Inaccessible Pinnacles' of the list: Stac Lee and Stac an Armin, in the St Kilda archipelago. These are two enormous sea-stacks, rising almost vertically from the sea, requiring matchless seamanship and rock climbing skills to approach and scale. Both have attitude in bucketloads, but I have not classed them as Hughs – why? Because they are stacks, not islands. But they are still surrounded by water, I hear people say. Yes, an island is a piece of land completely surrounded by water, but not every piece of land surrounded by water is necessarily an island. If this was the case, then every rock or skerry would be an island, regardless of size.

For this reason, I have also not included the Old Man of Hoy in Orkney or even the Bass Rock, off Scotland's east coast. Admittedly, this last example may be stretching things a bit too far, but its name justifies it being a rock and not an island. Perhaps its status as an important bird reserve, with associated restrictions on landing and climbing have also played a part in its omission as a Hugh.

Returning to St Kilda, which consists of a disparate collection of six islands, stacks and rocks, after much deliberation I arrived at four Hughs, notably Conachair, Oisebhal and Mullach Bi on the main island of Hirta and Mullach an Eilein on Boreray, easily the most prominent and striking of all the Hughs – and this is an understatement. The fact that landing on Boreray requires permission and direct intervention from the National Trust for Scotland (NTS) and is only possible in unusually calm conditions, at times when seabird disturbance is at a minimum, is the main reason I have not yet been to Boreray. It remains my one unclimbed Hugh but is on my bucket list.

There are still, arguably, some omissions to the island Hughs list which could warrant further explanation. I could preempt this potential discussion by mentioning two other St Kilda islands (Soay and Dun), Bac Mòr (The Dutchman's Cap) in the Treshnish Isles and the distant island of Rona. The above potential Hughs were indeed considered, but rejected for various reasons, the main one being that, in general, only islands which tend to have reasonable public access are included in this book. Scarba, Mingulay and, in particular, Boreray are obvious exceptions.

The Appeal of the Hughs

The bulk of Scottish hillwalkers tend to start on the Munros, before moving onto Corbetts and then Grahams. The more discerning, however, do not concentrate entirely on one list at a time, but simultaneously work through several lists, perhaps climbing all the best hills first. I don't know of anyone who has climbed all the Munros but never ascended say, Stac Pollaidh, The Cobbler or Arthur's Seat, but, knowing some people's obsessive addiction to Munros, I would bet there are a few in this category.

The beauty of the Hughs is that they have been chosen for their character, views and attitude and are consequently worth climbing. Their relatively low height ensures that the majority of them are easily approachable and accessible, especially to novices and children who may just be embarking on their hill-walking careers. Therefore, in a sense, it may seem more logical to be introduced to the hills by climbing a few Hughs, rather than starting on Munros.

Indeed, my own introduction to hillwalking was on a lowly coastal hill in Ayrshire, standing proudly above Carleton Crescent, a row of holiday bungalows near the village of Lendalfoot, just south of Girvan. Blissful childhood holidays were spent there and I climbed this hill on countless occasions. It is not a Hugh, but does look across the sea to the first Hugh described in this book: Ailsa Craig.

To come to the point, try not to leave the Hughs until old age, or until completion of the other lists. Admittedly, the Hughs are an ideal objective for older hillwalkers, as well as children, but some of the more remote or inaccessible ones will require the bullishness of youth to overcome, especially Boreray in St Kilda! The 200 Hughs are a challenge for all ages and will provide magical memories to last a lifetime. In the words of Geoffrey Winthrop Young: 'Only a hill, but all of life to me, up there between the sunset and the sea' (from the poem 'A Hill').

Redefining the Grahams

Since Volume 1 of *The Hughs* was published, the class of Scottish hills known as the Grahams has undergone a change of criteria used to define the inclusion of a hill into the list. Originally defined as Scottish hills over 2,000ft and under 2,500ft, with 150m of re-ascent, the lower height threshold has now been metricised and lowered to 600m (1,968.5ft). This change has resulted in 12 new Grahams added to the original list, having heights between 1,968.5ft (600m) and 2,000ft (610m).

This change obviously affects the Hughs list, as a Hugh is a Scottish hill under 2,000ft (with attitude!) and therefore may, and indeed does, include some of these 12 hills. (See below for the hills affected in both Volume 1 and Volume 2 of *The Hughs*.)

The pertinent question as to how and why this change was made, is briefly discussed here. The original list of Grahams was created by Fiona Graham (originally Fiona Torbet) in 1992 and subsequently amended in the light of Alan Dawson's 'Relative

Hills of Britain', listing all summits in Britain having 150m of re-ascent (regardless of actual height), which he called 'Marilyns'. The resulting final list of Grahams was born through an amicable discussion between Fiona Graham and Alan Dawson and all seemed hunky dory… until 2022.

It was then that Alan Dawson decided to effect the above change, presumably to dovetail more harmoniously with current metric lists of British hills, such as 'Simms', a loose acronym for 600m summits with at least 30m of re-ascent. As Fiona Graham is now deceased, Alan has assumed the mantle of the instigator of the Grahams list and has lowered the original 610m (2,000 feet) to a rounder and crisper 600m (but not so crisp 1,968.5ft). On the one hand, this seems a sensible and obvious change, given we are allegedly becoming a metricated country… though there are few signs that kilometres are soon replacing miles.

The change itself is perhaps not as contentious as the retention of the name 'Grahams'. If, for instance, the Munros were redefined as Scottish mountains over 900m rather than 915m (3,000ft), would the name 'Munro' still be honestly applicable to this essentially new class of mountain, without doing a disservice to Hugh Munro himself? Fiona Graham may not be as prominent as Sir Hugh, but surely the original criteria for inclusion should remain sacrosanct. Incidentally, Dawson now refers to Scottish hills

over 2,000ft (with 150m of re-ascent) as 'Fionas'. In my opinion, the obvious course of action would have been to retain the ORIGINAL name 'Grahams' for the ORIGINAL list and to come up with a NEW name – 'Dawsons' (?) – for the new list of hills over 600m.

In conclusion, to provide continuity with Volume 1 of *The Hughs* and out of respect for the late Fiona Graham, this volume (and the first) adheres to the original definition of a Graham, as a Scottish mountain between 2,000ft and 2,500ft high. Thus, the acronym Hugh (Hills Under Graham Height) is obviously contingent on this adherence.

Affected Hills

For completeness, the following information indicates the Hughs having heights between 600m and 610m, which would cease to be Hughs if the above change in lower height threshold was adopted. Four Hughs would be affected: three in Volume 1 and one in Volume 2. The three in Volume 1 are: Sgorach Mòr (601m) in Argyll, Cruach nam Miseag (606m) in Argyll and Sidhean (or Sithean) Mòr (601m) in Morar. The one in Volume 2 is Thacla (or Hecla) (606m) in South Uist.

One other hill in Volume 1, namely The Coyles of Muick, was given a height of 601m, but following a re-survey, is now 599m and therefore firmly in the Hughs category! For anyone adopting the Dawson change, there are therefore now 196 Hughs rather than 200.

Key to Using this Guide

Information Boxes

Each route description is headed with an Information Box. This concisely itemises the following essential information:

- hill height in metres and in feet
- associated 1:50000 os map(s)
- 6-figure grid reference of the summit(s)
- total distance (including return height gain)
- estimated completion time(s)
- access point with grid reference
- difficulty
- summary

All of the Hughs are accessible, but the 'Difficulty' and 'Summary' sections in the Information Box provide a quick guide to the characteristics and challenges of individual hills.

Sketch Maps

Five location maps show the Hughs by region and each individual route is accompanied by a sketch map designed by the author to be as clear and uncluttered as possible. These maps could in principle be used 'in the field', but when walking it is advisable to have the appropriate os map.

Route Quality

The quality of a hill route is, to a large extent, subjective and may be affected by weather conditions, season, etc. The following criteria, satisfied in ratios varying from hill to hill, have been used to select the Hughs:

- prominence
- position
- panorama

Circular routes are generally more satisfying than 'there and back' walks and for each outing every effort has been made to avoid returning exactly the same way, wherever practicable. Possible alternative routes are also sometimes mentioned or described briefly.

Names of Hills

Where it appears, the derivation of a hill's name is given either in the Information Box or in the narrative describing the route. There is an index of hill names at the end of the book.

PART I

THE SOUTHERN ISLES AND INNER HEBRIDES — 50 HUGHS

THE FIRTH OF CLYDE AND KINTYRE — 4 HUGHS
ISLAY, JURA AND SURROUNDING ISLANDS — 9 HUGHS
MULL AND SURROUNDING ISLANDS — 8 HUGHS
TIREE AND THE SMALL ISLES — 4 HUGHS
SKYE AND RAASAY — 25 HUGHS

Ailsa Craig from the Ayrshire coast

Scrinadle (Jura) from Glen Batrick

THE FIRTH OF CLYDE AND KINTYRE – 13 HUGHS

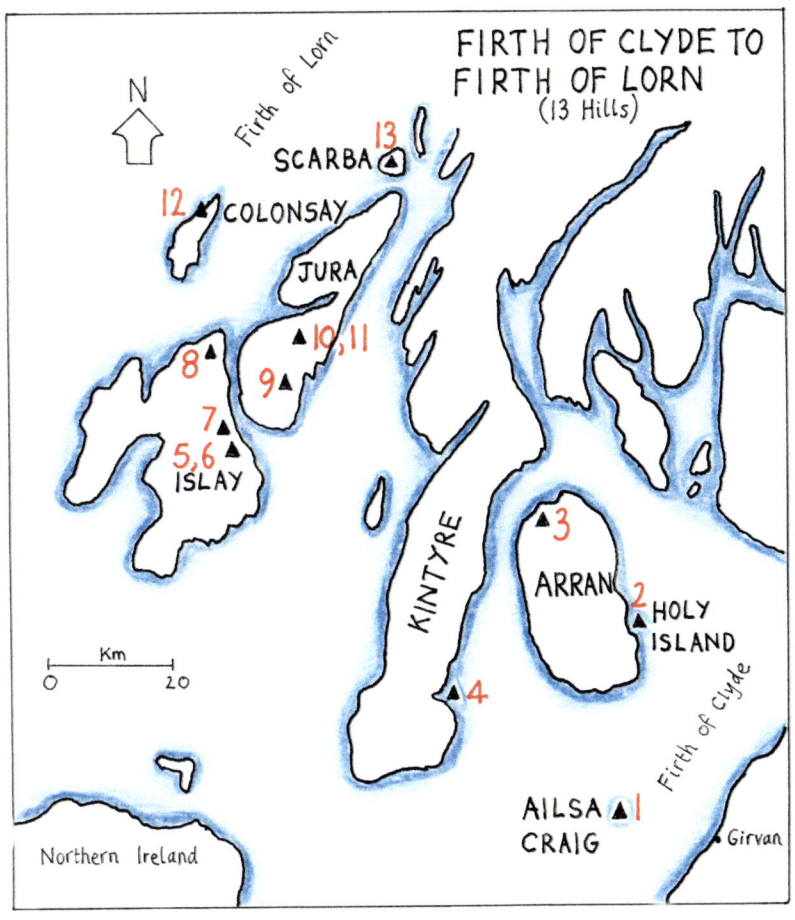

FIRTH OF CLYDE TO FIRTH OF LORN (13 Hills)

AILSA CRAIG

I. THE CAIRN (338M/1,109FT)

MAP	OS SHEET 76 (GR 019998)
DISTANCE	2KM
ASCENT	338M
TIME	1.5–2 HRS
ACCESS	THE PIER (SEE BELOW FOR AILSA CRAIG ACCESS)
DIFFICULTY	GOOD PATH TO THE CASTLE, BECOMING VERY OVERGROWN HIGHER UP
SUMMARY	Ailsa Craig is the epitome of the term 'island mountain', and a classic island Hugh in every sense. Its thrusting ramparts of ancient rock rear directly out of the sea to form a spellbinding, distinctive cone which almost begs to be climbed.

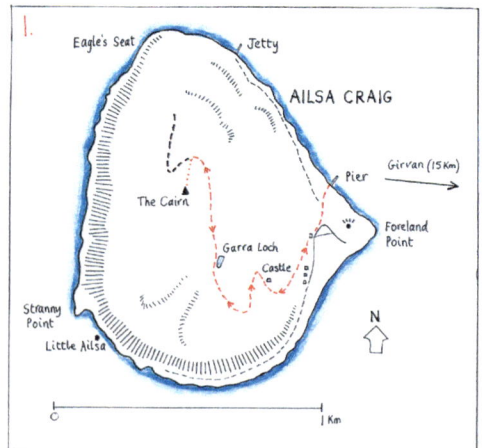

AILSA CRAIG IS a remarkable volcanic plug situated in the Firth of Clyde about 18km south of Arran and 16km from the Ayrshire coast at Girvan. Its exceptional profile makes it an obvious feature for miles around and is colloquially known as Paddy's Milestone, being halfway by sea from Glasgow to Belfast. The name Ailsa Craig literally means 'Fairy Rock'.

My own personal attachment to Ailsa Craig dates far back to my earliest childhood, from when we spent regular summer holidays at the village of Lendalfoot on the Ayrshire coast. 'The Craig' has always occupied a special place in my heart and has almost become an icon of childhood.

Ailsa Craig's south and west faces are almost a continuous bastion of precipitous cliffs presenting an air of impregnability and it is only on the east side that gentler slopes lead down to the sheltered nose of Foreland Point. Here are the pier, lighthouse and

Approaching Ailsa Craig

cluster of ruined quarrymen's cottages together with the rusting remains of the old narrow-gauge railway serving the quarries. The island's fine micro granite was mined to make world famous curling stones until the mid-20th century.

Unsurprisingly, Ailsa Craig is a renowned bird sanctuary, home to a diverse array of species including puffins, guillemots, kittiwakes and a vast gannet population.

The only easy route to the summit of Ailsa Craig is from the east side where an initially well-defined path zigzags up to a ruined castle, before becoming less distinct in the upper reaches. It is advisable to allow 2 hours for the round trip up and down, although most people would accomplish this in little over an hour. Most tour operators allow at least 2 hours on the island.

Once ashore, follow the old railway for a short distance to an old ramshackle building (the old tearoom) where the path climbs gently upwards to the left before swinging back right to arrive at the castle. This is at a height of 110m and already a third of the way to the top. The old square peel tower was built by the Hamilton family but few records remain as to its purpose or length of occupation.

The path beyond soon becomes choked with bracken but in spring and summer these upper slopes are festooned with wild flowers, namely campion, bluebells, harebells and sea thrift to name a few. The path again swings left and right and as you ascend the sense of height is sensational, the lighthouse and associated buildings looking like Lego toys.

The path soon enters a shallow depression to pass the tiny Garra Loch,

On Ailsa Craig

heading north over rock slabs passing below the summit before gradually swinging back to head south, finally reaching the natural stone trig point and small cairn.

On a clear day the summit panorama is exceptional, Arran, Kintyre, the Ayrshire coast and even Ireland being visible. The on-top-of-the-world feeling is quite profound and unique; who needs Everest?! Unfortunately, on my only ascent, a heat haze obliterated everything but the immediate area of sea.

Return by the route of ascent.

If you are lucky, as we were, you may get the chance to sail round the island before heading back to Girvan. This is a fantastic opportunity to view the immense western cliffs and bird life and should not be missed.

Getting to Ailsa Craig

Most boat trips run from Girvan, on the Ayrshire coast and the main operator is Mark McCrindle, 7 Harbour St, Girvan. He can be contacted by telephone on 01465 713219 or email mccrindle@aol.com. Another is ` JAG Charters Ltd (Tel: 01465 713174).

It is usually a four-hour round trip, allowing about 2 hours on Ailsa Craig which is ample time to climb to the top and back. It is also possible to sail from Arran, but these trips are longer and may not offer landing. Booking is standard.

HOLY ISLAND

2. MULLACH MÒR BIG TOP (314M/1,030FT)

MAP	OS SHEET 69 (GR 064297)
DISTANCE	6KM
ASCENT	314M
TIME	3–4 HRS
ACCESS	THE PIER (SEE BELOW FOR HOLY ISLAND ACCESS)
DIFFICULTY	SKETCHY ROUGH PATH WITH ONE SMALL SCRAMBLING SECTION BELOW SUMMIT
SUMMARY	Like Ailsa Craig, Mullach Mòr is a superb small island mountain forming a craggy summit and offering unmatched views of Arran's serrated skyline peaks.

ONE OF A number of islands in the UK which go under the name of Holy Island, Arran's little offshore neighbour is a haven of peace and solitude, yet only a 10-minute boat trip away from the hustle and bustle of Lamlash, on the east side of Arran.

The name derives from the island's long association with early Christianity, being the home of a sixth century Irish monk, St Molaise, who lived in a hermit's cave near a holy spring, still visible at GR 058297. The holy tradition has continued with the purchase of the island in 1992 by the Samye Ling Buddhist community who have successfully transformed the island into 'an environmental and spiritual sanctuary dedicated to world peace and health.'

The walk to be described ascends the hill by the north ridge and returns by the easy track along the west side passing the cave and the holy spring, making a pleasant and memorable circuit. Note that the east side of the island has precipitous crags and is reserved for rare breeds of wild animals and should be given a wide berth.

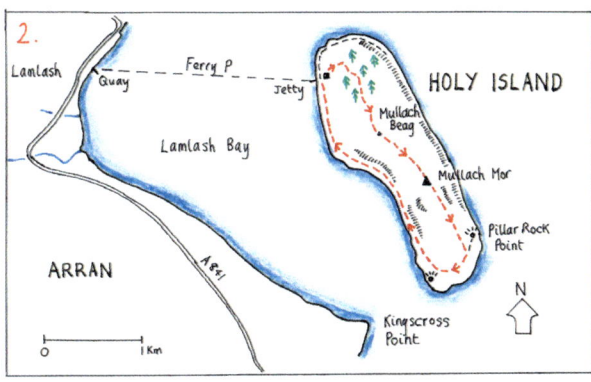

Holy Island from Arran

After landing on the island you will no doubt be met by a representative from the Centre for World Peace and Health who, incidentally, offer retreats and visits. First impressions of the island are the large White House (the Buddhist Centre), mini Buddhist stupas and fluttering prayer flags.

Head left from the pier and through a gap between two Tibetan flags into a large field. Various signs indicating 'To the Top' are a helpful crutch for any lost souls. Cross a stile at the top of the field and enter an area of recently planted forest of mainly birch and rowan trees. The trust has planted an amazing 35,000 mature trees on the island's north side and the path winds its way up through here onto the heathery northwest shoulder of the wee subsidiary top of Mullach Beag (Little Top). Another stile is crossed and an often-muddy path leads to the minor top of Mullach Beag crowned by a large cairn. If you are lucky, you may have already spotted some of the island's resident Soay sheep and even wild Eriskay ponies and bearded Saanen goats, though the latter tend to hang out on the east side.

Drop slightly to a col then continue to follow the ridge up a small, steep craggy section involving a minor hands-on scramble… nothing too scary! The airy summit has a triangulation pillar (trig point) and is a marvellous vantage point – the perfect excuse for a long and leisurely lunch stop, unless the local midgies are out in force.

Continue south from the summit

On Mullach Mòr

following the path down a steepish craggy ridge, levelling out on a broad heathery shoulder. From here there is a fine view of Ailsa Craig's pointed profile. Look out for a section of path passing between a roped-off area with danger signs warning of deep crevices and fissures on either side of the path.

Descending further, the lighthouse and associated buildings are visible to the right, now a Buddhist retreat centre. A little wooden chalet nestling in a hollow to the right is the home of Lama Yeshe Losal Rinpoche, the executive director of the Holy Island Project.

Reach the junction with the main coastal path where you may wish to turn left for a few hundred metres to view the other lighthouse at Pillar Rock Point. Follow the coast path right, leading round to the west coast past the lighthouse and retreat centre.

The path following the coast from here is on pleasant short grass and is a delightful stroll with wonderful views and plenty of points of interest includ-ing brightly coloured Buddhist rock paintings, the cave of St Molaise and the Holy Spring. Return to the pier and centre in a little under 3km.

Getting to Holy Island

Holy Island is easily reached by passenger ferry from the pier at Lamlash on Arran with the first sailing usually at 10am and the last return trip around 5pm. It is not usually necessary to book, but contact the Holy Island office on 01770 601100 if in doubt. The boat regularly transports people there and back all day and you may return anytime up to 5pm. Please note that dogs are not allowed on the island.

3. MEALL NAN DAMH ROUNDED HILL OF THE STAGS (570M/1,870FT)

MAP	OS SHEET 69 (GR 911469)
DISTANCE	12KM (SHORTER VARIATIONS – SEE TEXT)
ASCENT	1,030M
TIME	5–7 HRS
ACCESS	PIRNMILL
DIFFICULTY	SOME SCRAMBLING ON BEINN BHARRAIN (AVOIDABLE) – MAINLY EASY GRASS RIDGE WALKING
SUMMARY	Meall nan Damh is by far the most prominent and steep-sided sub-2,000ft peak on Arran. The described route, including the Graham of Beinn Bharrain is a superb high-level excursion.

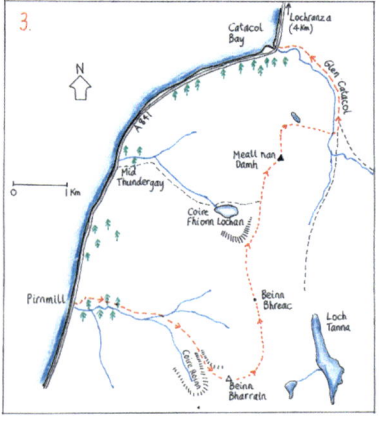

THE ISOLATED WEE hill of Meall nan Damh is situated in north Arran above Catacol Bay and is particularly noticeable from Claonaig on the Kintyre peninsula from where the ferry departs to Lochranza. It totally dominates the view looking south from Catacol Bay.

The hill can easily be climbed on its own from Catacol Bay as a possible round trip by Glen Catacol and a return by the north ridge (7km). The best hill-only option, however, is to ascend from Mid Thundergay by a good path to the unique Coire Fhionn Lochan, climb the hill then descend into Glen Catacol and return by the main road (a round trip of 12km).

Although the described route (including Beinn Bharrain) is also 12km, this does not include the longish road walk back to Pirnmill which would add another 7km. I was lucky enough to be deposited at Pirnmill by car and only had an extra 5km round to Lochranza where we had a holiday cottage.

At Pirnmill a farm track leads up the hill just north of the bridge. Follow this round a left, then a right bend until it again bends to the left. Leave the track here, crossing a stile to a muddy

Meall nan Damh

path through a coppice of birch and hazel trees. The path crosses another high stile, becoming established on the north side of the Allt Gobhlach (Forked Stream) set in a deep gorge with a fine waterfall. Higher up you will notice a new hydro track on the opposite side of the stream leading to a concrete weir.

Cross the stream at the weir and head for Coire Roinn (Dividing Corrie) enclosed by two obvious ridges. The left-hand ridge is steeper with some fine scrambling (the described route). The right-hand ridge is longer and gentler and leads to a subsidiary top of Beinn Bharrain. If scrambling is not your forte, then this ridge is the ideal alternative with an added bonus of bagging another summit!

The approach to the left-hand ridge is on huge granite slabs and heather, with scrambling beginning at an obvious outcrop marking the start of a narrow, more level section. Most difficulties can be avoided by grassy ledges on the right, but staying on the ridge crest offers the finest situations on a succession of granite steps. The scrambling ends all too soon and the summit triangulation pillar is just a short walk round to the left.

From the summit, descend north-eastwards to the bealach, enjoying grand views of Arran's highest hill loch (Loch Tanna – slender loch) and across to the main castelled Arran ridges to the east. A long gentle ascent leads to the subsidiary summit of Beinn Bhreac (Speckled Hill) where Meall nan Damh is seen to advantage. Descend north over a minor top and continue north along the ridge forming the eastern boundary of Coirein Lochain containing Coire Fhionn Lochan (Fair Lochan), an atmospheric hill lochan well worth

Meall nan Damh from Beinn Bhreac

a visit, where you may just spot a red-throated diver. A path descends to this loch at the base of the ridge.

A further descent takes you down to a tiny lochan nestling below the steep south-western flank of Meall nan Damh. From here, ascend the final 200m keeping to the left on slightly easier ground in deep heather to reach the large cairn at the summit. Not surprisingly, the views are splendid, especially down to Glen Catacol and Catacol Bay.

The described route returns by Glen Catacol to Catacol Bay, but if you have not arranged transport back to Pirnmill then an alternative is to descend to Mid Thundergay by the Coire Fhionn Lochan path from where it is less than 3km to Pirnmill.

To reach Glen Catacol, descend the north ridge of Meall nan Damh and swing round right by a small lochan before dropping down easy slopes to the glen. Cross the stream to reach a rough path on the opposite side. Glen Catacol is a beautiful, secluded little glen and provides a relaxing 2.5km walk to the road at Catacol Bay.

Getting to Arran

Arran is normally reached by car ferry from Ardrossan to Brodick (booking essential if you are coming by car) (Tel: 01770 302140).

A much cheaper and shorter crossing option is the car ferry from Claonaig (Kintyre) to Lochranza. No booking is required (Tel: 0871 2002233).

4. ISLAND DAVAAR SUMMIT (115M/377FT)

MAP	OS SHEET 68 (GR 757200)
DISTANCE	4.5KM
ASCENT	115M
TIME	1–2 HRS
ACCESS	LARGE LAY-BY OPPOSITE THE ISLAND
DIFFICULTY	AN EASY WALK ACROSS A SHINGLE STRAND FOLLOWED BY AN EQUALLY EASY GRASSY ASCENT
SUMMARY	A straightforward hike to the top of one of the few relatively large tidal islands off Scotland's coast.

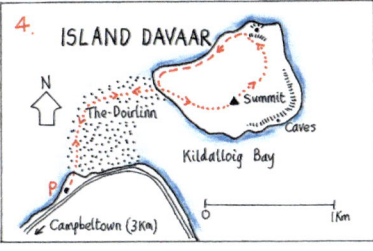

'ISLAND DAVAAR' IS an anglicised corruption of the Gaelic *Eilean Dà Bhàrr*, '*bhàrr*' meaning 'top point' or 'extremity, pertaining to the prominent nameless hill. It is a pertinent landmark sitting at the entrance to Campbeltown Loch on the west side of the Kintyre peninsula, its south-eastern edge presenting a steep bastion of red micro granite cliffs containing a series of caves. The largest of these contains the celebrated Crucifixion painting, something of a cultish tourist draw. Davaar bears more than a passing resemblance to Ailsa Craig, being of

comparable size and shape but only about a third of the height.

The island can be accessed by pedestrians via a dog-legged spit of shingle beach roughly 3 hours either side of low tide, giving a maximum six-hour window in which to visit the island. This is ample time to climb to the top and complete a circular coastal walk with a visit to the Crucifixion Cave. The described route is partly circular but is not a guide to the complete coastal circuit.

To reach the start, take the minor road from Campbeltown along the southern shore of Campbeltown Loch to a large lay-by just over 3km from Campbeltown itself. Various warning signs concerning the tide are dotted about and even at low tide there are often areas of shallow water that may require crossing. Generally, it is better to stay further left as you cross the Doirlinn, as it is known in Gaelic. 'Doirlinn' is literally 'an islet to which

Davaar

one can wade at low water; pebbly or stony part of a shore; an isthmus'. During the walk across you may spot waders and eider ducks. Reach the island in less than 1km.

There is no definitive route to the summit and any one of the various grassy paths meandering upwards through swathes of bracken and heather will take you to the top in around 20 minutes. The summit is fairly flat and crowned by a triangulation pillar.

Ailsa Craig's profile is quite pointed from this angle and Arran plus much of the Kintyre coastline is well seen. Campbeltown of course is laid out to the west.

To vary the descent, stay on high ground over two small hillocks heading north-east then north. Make a gradual descent to the lighthouse at the north of the island to pick up a track where you turn left, leading back to the point of ascent in less than 1km.

If you wish to visit the Crucifixion Cave, follow the coast around anti-clockwise on a good path initially, then a shingle beach and water-rounded boulders. The series of caves soon begin, some little more than large hollows in the cliff. The Crucifixion Cave has a double entrance on a wide grassy platform and directly faces Ailsa Craig (GR 760199).

The painting is high up and life-size, using irregularities in the rock to create a three-dimensional effect. Painted by local artist Alexander MacKinnon in 1887, it has since been retouched by the artist himself and by other local artists more recently.

ISLAY

5. GLAS BHEINN GREY HILL (472M/1,548FT)
6. BEINN BHEIGIER OBSCURE – POSSIBLY VICAR'S HILL (491M/1,612FT)

MAP	OS SHEET 60 (GR 429592, 430564)
DISTANCE	17KM
ASCENT	800M
TIME	5–7 HRS
ACCESS	ARDTALLA (CLAGGAIN BAY)
DIFFICULTY	ROUGH COASTAL PATH AND BROAD STONY MOUNTAIN RIDGES. GOOD NAVIGATION REQUIRED IF AT ALL MISTY
SUMMARY	A delightful and varied expedition traversing Islay's two highest peaks, with marvellous views across the Sound of Islay to the Paps of Jura.

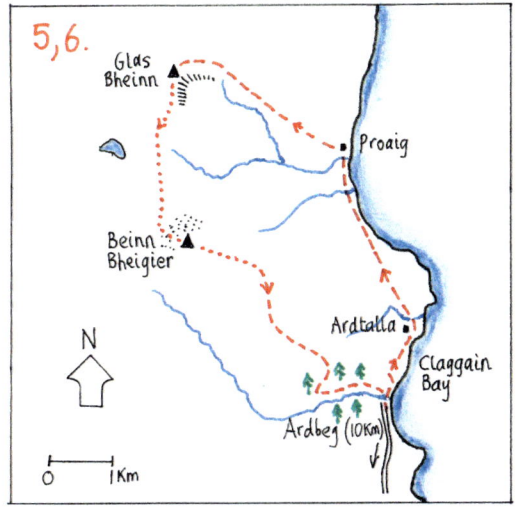

ALTHOUGH THE ISLAY hills lack the obvious 'in your face' attitude of their bolder Jura cousins across the water, they nevertheless display a distinct purity of form and individuality, as well as offering an almost limitless panorama of sea and hills.

These two hills, together with their northern neighbour of Sgòrr nam Faoileann (described separately) form the main hill group on the eastern side of Islay. These two are normally ascended from Ardtalla in the east but Glas Bheinn could be combined with Sgòrr nam Faoileann in an approach from Storakaig (see following route).

Start at the end of the minor road at Claggain Bay where there is a parking area on the right. This is about 10km from Ardbeg. Follow the partially tarmacked track to Ardtalla farm. Pass a holiday cottage and go through two gates before crossing a field and a stream. Bear left, going through another gate and descend through an area of scrubby bushes and trees. Soon, there is a fine view northwards of a wide bay and the wee cottage of Proaig.

Cross a stream and take the right fork beyond, ascending then descending to the coastline where the path improves significantly. Reach Proaig ('broad bay' in Old Norse) by crossing the burn on steppingstones. Though Proaig is a wonderfully remote settlement, in the 12th century the whole bay was one of the most prosperous on Islay when successive farms were built and worked by families and clan chiefs of the Lords of the Isles. Proaig itself was abandoned in the 1930s.

On older maps a path is shown heading north-west from Proaig and ascending Glas Bheinn's prominent south-east ridge. It leaves the ridge to reach the col between Glas Bheinn and Sgòrr nam Faoileann before making a gradual descent to Storakaig to the north-west. Time and lack of use have made this path at best intermittent and at worst non-existent.

However, this provides the line of ascent up this south-east ridge, fairly grassy to start, then gradually becoming steeper and stonier as you gain height. The rock is hard quartzite which in wet conditions can be quite slippery. Just beyond a final steepening, the ridge curves south-west to the summit with its several cairns.

Enjoy a fine view of the next peak of Beinn Bheigier almost 3km directly south across complex terrain.

From the summit, traverse an almost level section of ridge past bands of quartzite overlooking some small lochans on the west side. In clear weather the route over the subsidiary peak of Am Mam is fairly obvious but two branching spurs heading east and west provide a false lure for the unwary in thick weather.

The route bears west for a short distance before following the main ridge over Am Mam, a confusing section of knolls and troughs.

Descend to the bealach and gain the west ridge of Beinn Bheigier by heading slightly to the right. This avoids most of the scree covering the northern slopes of the hill. Climb to the summit on tongues of grass and heather. At the top is a trig point with a surrounding shelter cairn and is a great spot to linger, enjoying the wide-ranging views with the Paps of Jura stealing the show.

The descent route follows the hill's long south-east ridge over several minor

Glas Bheinn from the summit of Beinn Bheigier

tops – a fine high-level walk. After 1km, aim for an obvious cairn to the right marking the route down the southern spur, which develops into a vague grassy path. Lower down, beware of false trails heading east rather than south-east.

Reach a section of constructed track and go through a gate into an area of newly planted trees. This track and planted area are very recent and not shown on older maps. Turn right and follow the track west until it hairpins back east going through two more gates to finally reach the road at Claggain Bay and the starting point.

7. SGÒRR NAM FAOILEANN ROCKY PEAK OF THE BEACH (429M/1,407FT)

MAP	OS SHEET 60 (GR 432607)
DISTANCE	8KM
ASCENT	370M
TIME	3–4 HRS
ACCESS	STORAKAIG TRACK END (GR 402625)
DIFFICULTY	VERY INDISTINCT PATH ON TUSSOCKY TERRAIN FOLLOWED BY A BROAD ROCKY RIDGE
SUMMARY	Arguably the shapeliest and certainly the rockiest hill on Islay with dramatic summit views superior to Beinn Bheigier.

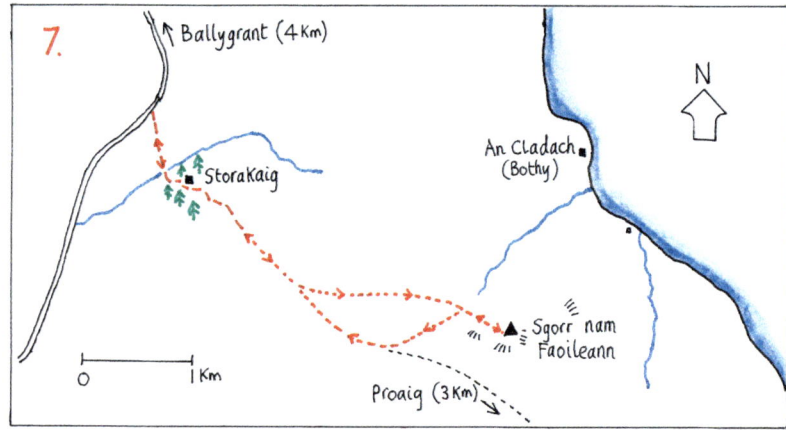

FOR MANY WALKERS completing the previous route, this hill gets pushed onto the back burner with the tag of 'must do this hill on a future occasion'. Some never get round to it, but the lucky ones who do discover that this hill may just be the best on Islay, not just in terms of its fine rocky profile, but for the sheer quality of its summit panorama.

Many a time have I chugged past this coastal eminence on the ferry to Port Askaig and gazed spellbound up its craggy north-eastern ramparts with a longing to climb it. Indeed, if you are prepared for a longer walk or are lucky enough to stay at the Mountain Bothy

Approaching Sgòrr nam Faoileann

Association (MBA) bothy of An Cladach (The Stony Beach) at the hill's foot on the seaward side, then the circuit of Gleann Ghàireasdail via the summit would be a marvellous outing.

For lesser mortals, however, the somewhat featureless approach from Storakaig on what used to be a reasonable path but now largely non-existent, is the quickest route to the top. Reach Storakaig by the minor road from Ballygrant heading south across featureless back country. This road is signposted Cluanach and eventually joins the minor road connecting Bridgend and Port Ellen.

Four kilometres from Ballygrant is the entrance to Storakaig farmhouse set in a copse of trees down a track.

Dunlossit Estates have seen fit recently to adopt permanent signs on gates indicating that 'Stalking is in progress' and to seek an alternative route or phone the Estate Office. As stalking normally only takes place from mid-August to December (or February), for about half the year this sign is nonsense. There is also no stalking on a Sunday – at any time. Regardless of your view, the sign is very walker-unfriendly and has undoubtedly deterred many people approaching from this point.

On contacting the Estate Office concerning this sign I was given the reason that the comment refers to a blanket coverage of other activities such as chemical spraying, deer management

Jura from Sgorr nam Faoileann

Summit cairn of Sgorr nam Faoileann

to the right over boggy ground. The general line then follows higher ground to the left in a roughly south-easterly direction on an extremely sketchy path.

Aim directly for the fairly obvious west ridge of the hill, with the terrain becoming less tiresome as you gain height. Once above 300m, the broad ridge holds a profusion of quartzite slabs and low crags to add interest to the ascent. The final summit cone is a fine climb through a maze of craggy outcrops and the substantial summit cairn is perched precariously on one such outcrop.

There is a marvellous on-top-of-the-world feel to this spot with the sparkling waters of the Sound of Islay far below backed by the Paps of Jura beyond. Savour the moment.

Note that the neighbouring peak of Glas Bheinn could easily be added to the itinerary via a high bealach to the south-west. Otherwise, return by the route of ascent or drop down to pick up the 'path'.

counts, habitat monitoring etc. The sign wording may be changed to reflect this, but I'm not holding my breath.

To add salt to the wound, parking is a major problem on the narrow road and I had to go a further half kilometre or so to find a space.

The track bypasses the house on the right-hand side through two very awkward gates and follows the perimeter of the copse to a stile over the fence. Cross the stile and head down a grassy slope

8. SGARBH BREAC SPECKLED CORMORANT (364M/1,195FT)

MAP	OS SHEET 60 (GR 406766)
DISTANCE	16KM (SHORTER VARIATIONS POSSIBLE)
ASCENT	380M
TIME	5–7 HRS
ACCESS	BUNNAHABHAIN
DIFFICULTY	INTERMITTENT COASTAL PATH. NO DISCERNIBLE PATHS ON HIGHER GROUND
SUMMARY	A fine circular route on Islay's relatively unfrequented north-eastern extremity, culminating in the prominent dome of Sgarbh Breac.

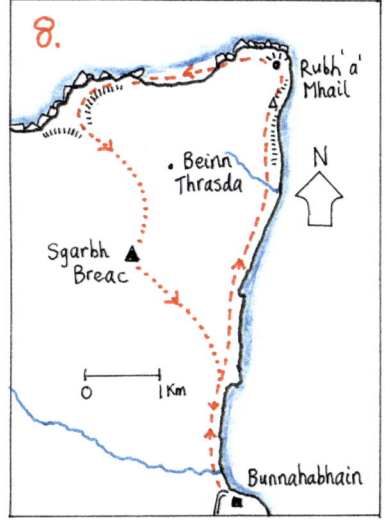

SGARBH BREAC RISES proudly from the wild tract of land forming Islay's north-eastern peninsula. It is well seen from the Port Askaig ferry, its conical profile arresting the eye.

The route to be described is by no means the shortest but takes the opportunity to explore some of the spectacular coastal scenery lying north and north-east of the hill.

Start at the Bunnahabhain distillery at the end of the minor road running north from the A846 Port Askaig road. Park in a small grassy parking area on the left just before the hairpin bend leading down to the distillery. Alternatively, park at the distillery visitors' car park where there is an excellent view of Sgarbh Breac.

A track goes left from the parking area for about 200m before turning right past an old World War II pill box. Follow this track and go through a gate before descending to cross the river by a footbridge (unmarked on some maps). Climb steeply up the other side on a gravel track to reach a reasonable ATV

Sgarbh Breac from Bunnahabhain

track heading north parallel to the shore following a line of telegraph poles. A good rhythm can be found on this track all the way to Gleann Dubh, a good 4km distant.

For those choosing not to explore the coastline, this point provides a good starting point for the ascent of Sgarbh Breac over its north-east shoulder of Beinn Thrasda.

The described route continues northwards, crossing the gorge of Gleann Dubh and descending to the shoreline to reach an old stone storage hut and jetty just before the lighthouse at Rubh' a'Mhàil, the north-eastern extremity of Islay.

The next 3km are a veritable goldmine of coastal delights including natural arches, raised beaches, caves, stacks, rock formations and a peppering of idyllic sandy beaches – a paradise for lovers of untamed, dramatic coastal scenery. The route is not described in detail so as not to detract from the exploratory nature of the walk.

At Port a'Chotain, some 3km on, there is a high, grassy raised beach with a multi-entrance cave system, left high and dry after Islay rose up several hundred feet following the last ice age. This is the point to head inland to Coir' Odhar where vague deer tracks lead up to Bealach Gaoth' Niar, the col separating Sgarbh Breac from Beinn Thrasda. From here follow the heathery north ridge to the summit, crowned by a trig point. The view from this airy, coastal perch is, not surprisingly, quite stunning, with the ubiquitous Paps of Jura arresting your gaze to the east.

Descend south-eastwards on broad, easy-angled slopes leading directly to the ATV track used on the outward journey. It is little over an hour from the summit to the car park at Bunnahabhain.

GETTING TO ISLAY

Regular sailings from Kennacraig (Kintyre) to Port Ellen or Port Askaig. Booking is essential unless you are travelling as a passenger (Tel: 08000 66 5000).
Regular air service from Glasgow (Tel: 0870 850 9850).

JURA

9. GLAS BHEINN GREY HILL (562M/1,844FT)

MAP	OS SHEET 61 (GR 500699)
DISTANCE	12KM
ASCENT	700M
TIME	4–6 HRS
ACCESS	CRAIGHOUSE (FOR JURA ACCESS SEE END OF ROUTE 10/11)
DIFFICULTY	NO DISTINCT PATHS BUT EASY, MAINLY GRASSY TERRAIN
SUMMARY	Glas Bheinn is an unfairly neglected wee hill offering unrivalled views of the Paps. Its traverse, including the southern satellite of Dubh Bheinn (Black Hill) is a grand outing.

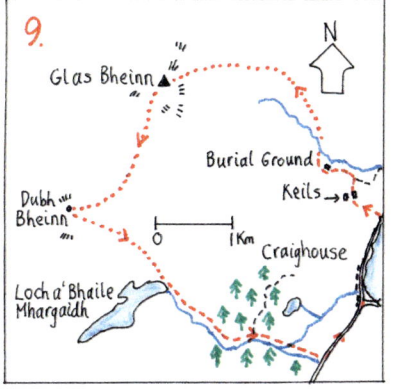

JURA IS DESERVEDLY known for its three distinctive scree domes known as the Paps of Jura, and for most hillwalkers these ankle-breaking brutes of hills are the island's main attraction. However, for the real hill connoisseur not blinkered by the magic 2,000ft contour, there are a host of smaller summits ripe for exploration.

Glas Bheinn is the most accessible of these, standing almost directly above the island's main centre of population at Craighouse. It is connected by a fine high-level ridge to Dubh Bheinn, the most southerly 500m summit on the island.

Begin by walking north from Craighouse along the A846 for 1km before taking the left turn along a minor road to Keils. Turn left again at a junction to reach the old burial ground. A metal gate at the rear of the cemetery leads on to a track passing the Water Treatment Works. Beyond here cross the stream on your right at a suitable point and make a rising traverse up easy grass slopes to reach the broad eastern spur of Glas Bheinn. In damp conditions, the going here can be quite boggy but improves as you gain the wide ridge crest.

Once established on the ridge, contin-

The Paps of Jura from Glas Bheinn

ue west up steeper, craggier terrain with several false summits until you reach the true summit marked with a substantial cairn. This viewpoint is one of the few places on Jura where all three Paps display their individual form, unless of course they are shrouded in low cloud which is often the case.

To continue southward to Dubh Bheinn simply follow the broad ridge over grass, heather, crowberry and endless rocky outcrops to the lowest point on the ridge where a tiny idyllic lochan nestles serenely in the wild landscape – a haunting spot.

The gentle ascent to Dubh Bheinn passes other tiny lochan and the summit sits on a plinth of metamorphic quartz-ite crowned by a trig pillar: another marvellous viewpoint.

To make a fine circuit, descend Dubh Bheinn's easy south-eastern flank to Loch a' Bhaile-Mhargaidh, a large hill loch. The name means 'Market Loch' and refers to the fact that cattle from Islay en route to markets at Crieff and Stirling swam across the Sound of Islay to Feolin and walked over the hills by this loch to Small Isles Bay near Keils.

Pass the loch's eastern end and follow its outflow down to a small bridge where a vague path continues down into a felled forestry area. Reach a forestry track passing a tall standing stone, leading to the main road in 1km. Turn left and reach Craighouse in under 1km.

10. SCRINADLE MEANING UNCERTAIN, BUT SEE BELOW (508M/1,667FT)
11. CORRA BHEINN POINTED HILL (575M/1,886FT)

MAP	OS SHEET 61 (GR 505778, 526755)
DISTANCE	15KM
ASCENT	825M
TIME	6–8HRS
ACCESS	START OF 'EVANS WALK' (GR 550732). FOR JURA ACCESS SEE END
DIFFICULTY	VERY BOGGY APPROACH PATH; THEREAFTER ROUGH WALKING AND SOME SCRAMBLING.
SUMMARY	The shapely Corra Bheinn, sometimes known as the fourth Pap, together with the remote coastal gem of Scrinadle give a memorable but demanding walk.

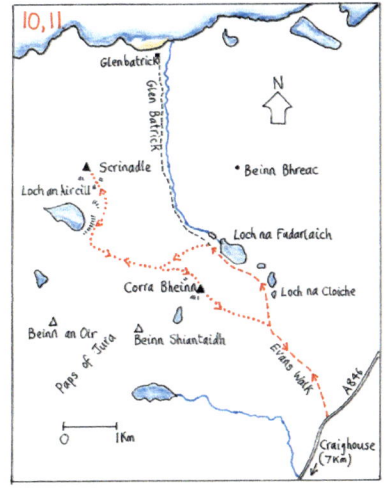

EXCLUDING THE PAPS, these two classic wee hills are arguably the finest on Jura. Indeed, if isolation and lack of people are high on your list then the pair will easily surpass the 'big three'.

The name 'Scrinadle' is unusual with possible Norse roots, though may derive from the Gaelic 'sgreanach' (rough, stormy) and 'adhbhal' (vast, awful). Being in such an exposed, coastal situation, the rough and stormy description is certainly apt.

Park in the large lay-by on the right side of the road about 1km north of the three arched bridge over the Corran River. If you don't have a car, the local Jura bus will drop you off at this point (7km north of Craighouse).

The start of the 'Evans Walk' to Glenbatrick on the island's west side begins here. The path was constructed by the late Mr Evans in the late 19th century in order to provide pony access to remote Glenbatrick. Though one of

The summit of Scrinadle

the few walking paths on the island, it is notoriously wet and boggy in sections – be prepared!

Cross the road and go over a plank bridge across a ditch. Walk a short distance to a sign indicating the Evans Walk beyond where the path forks. The right branch is higher (and drier!) but both branches meet again at a stream crossing. Continue along the boggy trail and cross a further two streams before the path starts to climb significantly, thankfully crossing firmer, drier ground.

Note that the easiest ascent of Corra Bheinn can be accomplished from here, but the described route ascends Scrinadle first before tackling the much steeper north ridge of Corra Bheinn involving some scrambling. If scrambling doesn't appeal then either climb Corra Bheinn now, returning to the Evans path, or leave it until the walk out.

Pass Loch na Cloiche on your right before reaching the high point of the Evans Walk looking down on Loch na Fùdarlaich, a marvellous wild spot. The path skirts the west side of this loch before gradually descending for 4km to the remote Glenbatrick lodge on the coast. Although not the described route, purists who wish to accomplish a complete traverse of Scrinadle could descend to Glenbatrick before making a long, leisurely ascent of the knobbly north-east ridge.

The described route contours round the northern flank of Corra Bheinn after passing the loch, crosses a stream and ascends easy slopes to the bealach on Scrinadle's south ridge. From here it is a gradual climb on grass and rocky outcrops to the summit with grand views of the fine glaciated Loch an Aircill below on the left.

The summit cairn of Scrinadle is a superb spot to linger enjoying delectable sea views out to the island of Colonsay. There is a palpable feeling of delicious remoteness on this absolute gem of a hill.

For those averse to retracing steps, it would be quite possible to make a long descent of Scrinadle's north-east ridge to Glenbatrick and return by the Evans Walk. However, the described route returns down the south ridge to the bealach with its two little lochans. From here there is a fine view of Corra

Corra Bheinn from the coll

Bheinn's northern aspect of quartzite slabs, boulders and crags.

From the bealach, descend gradually to the right, crossing two streams to reach the lower slopes of Corra Bheinn. The initial two thirds of the ascent is generally fairly benign, following easier ground to the left of a line of crags. Further up the going steepens considerably, and some hands-on scrambling is unavoidable, choosing any number of possible routes. Watch out for loose blocks and be very aware if the rock is at all wet.

Finally, the angle eases and you reach the mountain's multi-topped summit ridge. The actual summit is the most south-easterly top from where there is a fine view of Beinn Shiantaidh, the most easterly Pap.

Descend the easy south-eastern flank of the hill to reach the Evans Walk in just over 1km and return to the road.

GETTING TO JURA

The ferry to Jura leaves from Port Askaig (Islay) and sails to Feolin on Jura. The ferry is a 'turn up and go' (i.e. no need to book).

COLONSAY

12. CARNAN EOIN IAN'S CAIRN OR BIRD CAIRN (143M/469FT)

MAP	OS SHEET 61 (GR 409984)
DISTANCE	3KM
ASCENT	150M
TIME	1 HR
ACCESS	KILORAN BAY
DIFFICULTY	ONE OF THE SHORTEST, EASIEST ASCENTS IN THIS BOOK. OPTIONAL SCRAMBLING
SUMMARY	The rugged and rocky peak of Carnan Eoin is the highest point of Colonsay, beautifully situated at the end of a wonderful white beach. This gem of a hill almost begs to be climbed.

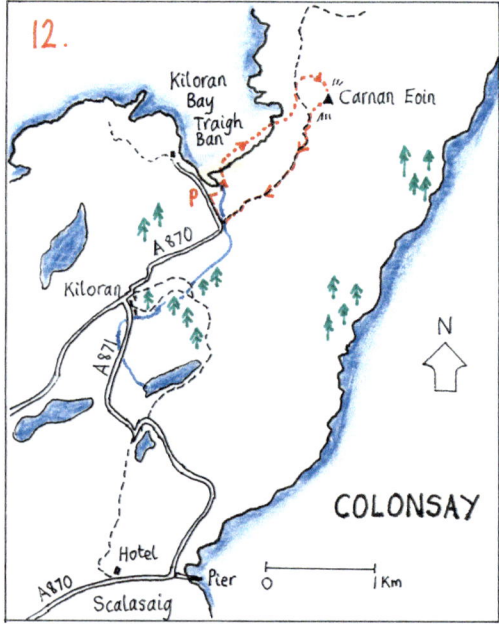

LYING NORTH OF Islay and west of Jura, the island of Colonsay largely escaped the ravages of the Clearances and latterly that of mass tourism. Its huge variety of landscapes, flora and fauna all packed into a relatively small area bestow it with a magic and tranquillity personifying the very essence of natural island beauty.

The whole island is remarkably rugged and is home to a host of craggy wee hills displaying an almost Torridonian quality. Unlike some islands where highest is not necessarily

Carnan Eoin and Traigh Ban

best, on Colonsay the highest hill is arguably the finest, though this should not be taken as a signal to ignore the others. Colonsay is an island perfect for individual exploration, so take the opportunity to do this.

Although the ferry to Colonsay from Oban is a vehicle ferry, many visitors elect to leave cars behind and hire bikes at Scalasaig or resort to Shanks' pony. It is a 4.5km road walk or cycle from Scalasaig to Kiloran Bay, but a better option if walking is to take the track through the hills beginning just west of the hotel and reaching the road again near a small lochan. This cuts out a large dogleg. From here another track leads to the small hamlet of Kiloran but this time the road is the quickest option.

If you do have a car, there is a parking area at the end of the public road just south of Kiloran Bay.

The view across Tràigh Ban (white beach) to the craggy terraces of Carnan Eoin at its north end is delightful and probably the definitive picture postcard image of the island.

The beach can be reached by entering a gate and crossing a small stream. Walk along the pristine sand for almost 1km before crossing another small stream to gain the lower slopes of the hill. For adventurous or impatient souls, a direct ascent can be made by a scramble up the cracks, crags and ledges of the south face on a variety of possible routes. A gentler ascent follows a track round west of the hill before leaving

Traigh Ban from Carnan Eoin

it to climb grassy slopes and small outcrops.

All too soon you reach the summit trig pillar and cairn from where much of the island is spread out before you. The view back along the sands is very fine. I spent very little time on the summit as I had left my better half sitting on a rock at the opposite end of the beach! She had organised a surprise weekend on Colonsay, staying at the hotel… bless her.

The return can be varied by following the aforementioned track back to the end of the road.

GETTING TO COLONSAY

Vehicle ferry from Oban six times a week (Tel: 01631 566688). • Vehicle ferry from Kennacraig (Kintyre) via Port Askaig (Islay) on Wed and Sat (Tel: 01880 730253). • Caravans/campervans allowed with permission only. There is an island post bus and bike hire.

SCARBA

13. CRUACH SCARBA STACK OR HEAP OF THE ROUGH ISLE (449M/1474FT)

MAP	OS SHEET 55 (GR 691045)
DISTANCE	10KM (SHORTER ROUTE POSSIBLE – 7KM)
ASCENT	500M
TIME	3.5–5 HRS / 2.5–4 HRS
ACCESS	JETTY (POLL NA H-EALAIDH) (720060) (SEE END FOR ACCESS TO SCARBA)
DIFFICULTY	A MIXTURE OF TRACK, PATH AND VERY ROUGH WALKING
SUMMARY	An adventurous ascent of a mountain rising directly from the sea. Beguiling views of a host of islands from its summit.

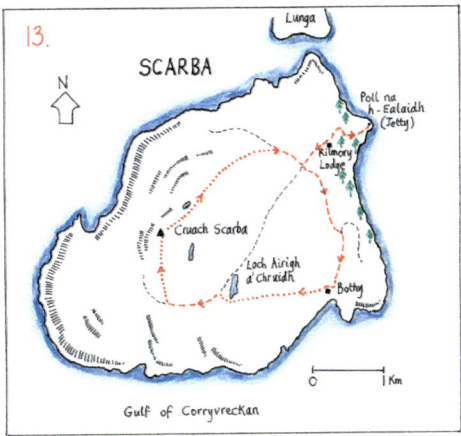

SCARBA IS AN island straight out of a *Boy's Own* adventure story – wild, uninhabited, rarely visited, separated from Jura in the south by the cataclysmic whirlpool of the Corryvreckan (speckled cauldron) and from Lunga in the north by the equally impressive and fearsome 'Grey Dog' tide run.

The east side of the island is relatively sheltered with native oak woodland and a large house known as Kilmory Lodge, occasionally used by the owner's family and friends. Near the lodge is a restricted little jetty north of a small promontory and the only safe landing place on the island. In the south, above a sheltered little bay sits a small cottage, used for a time as an adventure school for children and now an open bothy. Most of the south, and all of the west coast is a continuous stretch of crags, cliffs, waterfalls, raised beaches and caves – a veritable wonderland for adventurous souls.

The author on Cruach Scarba

The route to be described is circular and includes a visit to the bothy at the south of the island. If you are spending a night on the island then this will probably be your accommodation and, indeed, was my choice. For those with limited time, a direct there-and-back route from the jetty would be the best option.

From the jetty, a rough track leads uphill to Kilmory Lodge and just beyond here the track forks. Take the left branch contouring round the east side of the island and descend to a tiny, sheltered bay containing the un-named bothy. If you are doing the quick ascent, then take the right fork which is part of the return route.

The bothy occupies a gloriously tranquil location looking out over the bay and is a spacious five-room affair with table, chairs and camp beds. When I took residence in 2008 there were photos of children in outdoor gear, betraying its prior function as an outdoor centre.

From the bothy, ascend the hillside to the west on grass, heather and bracken, before descending slightly to cross a stream. From here, ascend again to eventually reach Loch Airigh a' Chruidh (loch in the horseshoe-shaped pasture), a beautifully wild spot.

Just above the loch join a path which circles its way around part of the island. Follow the path west as it contours its way round. After about 1km, leave the path to head uphill. (Beyond this point

Lunga from Cruach Scarba

the path descends to peter out above a steep gully). Easy slopes interspersed with quartzite ribs and crags lead quickly to the summit trig point and stone shelter.

The finest view is to the north, where a shimmering sea is punctuated by a flotilla of small islands, including Lunga, Rubha Fiola and the Garvellachs.

After believing myself to be the sole island occupant, I was most taken aback to meet a bunch of schoolchildren and staff near the summit, all from a private school in Rugby. They had been camping here for two nights and were currently based at the Rubha Fiola Outdoor Centre. Thankfully, they soon departed and I had this magical spot to myself. My diary records: 'must be the finest view I've had from any summit – a glittering sea, a pleasant breeze, sun and no midges – heaven!' Amen to that.

The best descent route is to head north-east down an obvious spur, passing a small lochan. The view to the north continues to tantalise as you saunter down, sometimes on excellent quartzite slabs. In less than 2km meet a path where you turn right. In only a few hundred metres reach the track junction mentioned on the outward journey. Follow the track down to the jetty and your starting point.

The bothy on Scarba

GETTING TO SCARBA

I secured the services of 'Seafari' who run trips to Corryvreckan from Easdale on a rigid inflatable boat (RIB) with horse seats and handrails. They offered to deposit me on the island and pick me up the following day.

Other Services: Farsain Cruises, Craobh (Tel: 01852 500664) • Gemini Cruises, Crinan (Tel: 01456 830208).

MULL TO RUM – 12 HUGHS

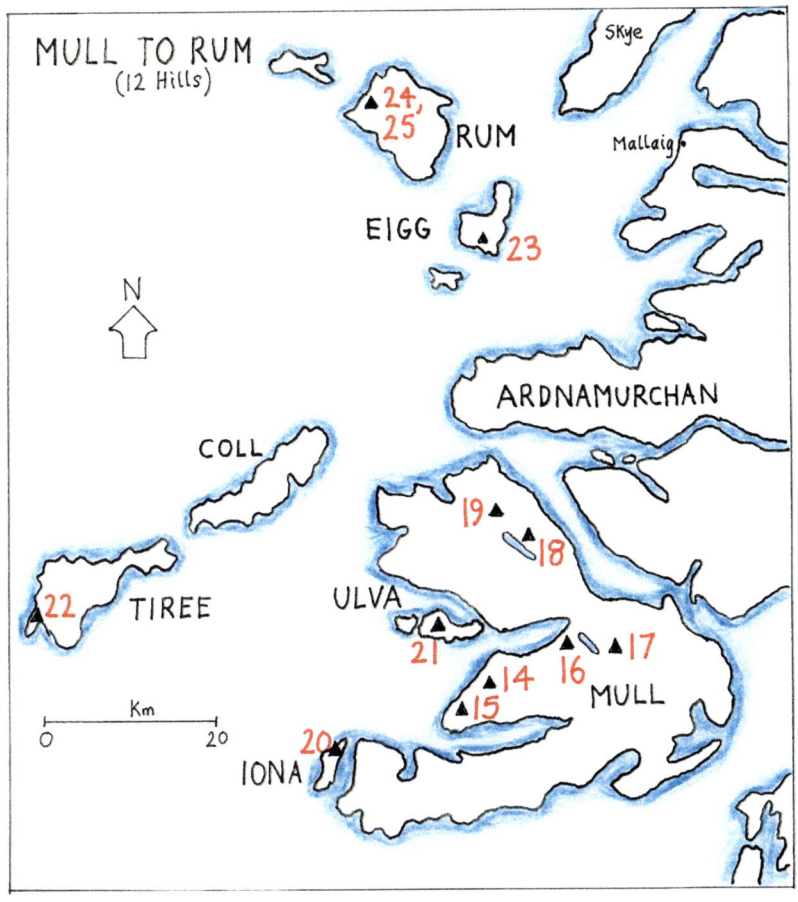

14. BEINN NA SREINE HILL OF BRIDLE/RESTRAINT (521M/1,710FT)
15. CREACH BHEINN HILL OF SPOIL (491M/1,611FT)

MAP	OS SHEET 48 (GR 456303, 419291)
DISTANCE	13KM
ASCENT	600M
TIME	4–6 HRS
ACCESS	B8035 ROAD (GR 455329) (FOR MULL ACCESS SEE END OF MULL ROUTES)
DIFFICULTY	NO PATHS; BOGGY IN PLACES
SUMMARY	These two delightful wee hills situated on the wild, western Ardmeanach peninsula cry out to be climbed on a summer's evening when the setting sun provides a glorious, golden backdrop. The summit view from Creach Bheinn is simply breathtaking.

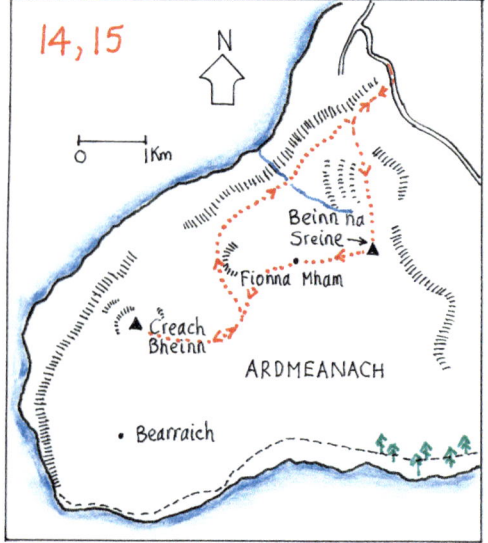

ALTHOUGH THE ARDMEANACH peninsula is renowned for its coastal features such as MacKinnon's Cave, the Fossil Tree and 'the wilderness', its wild interior culminating in the high point of Beinn na Sreine is an impressive, rock-strewn landscape inhabited only by deer, golden plover and the occasional golden eagle.

There is a small parking area on the north side of the B8035 below the long line of crags known as Creag a' Ghaill. Walk south-east along the road for a few hundred metres and cross the stream on the right to

Beinn na Sreine and Creach Bheinn from Ulva

gain access to the hill. Double back to follow the crest of Creag a' Ghaill on sheep-cropped grass, enjoying grand, panoramic views of the islands of Inch Kenneth and Ulva.

Before the line of cliffs begins to descend, head upwards through bands of rock to a level area with several tiny lochans. The map names this as Beinn na h-Iolaire (hill of the eagle). On my second ascent of this hill I saw no eagles but plenty of deer hinds and heard the constant peep-peep of plovers.

Continue south up a final rise through crags for 1km to reach the fairly substantial summit cairn of Beinn na Sreine. Although this hill has fine views, its westerly neighbour of Creach Bheinn is an even better viewpoint and epitomises the wild character of Ardmeanach.

Creach Bheinn lies almost 4km to the west over a broad, stony ridge, taking in the subsidiary top of Fionna Mham. As you near the dome of Creach Bheinn, there is a distinct 'edge-of-the-world' feeling with the sea closing in left and right. The final climb to the summit trig point passes through a complex tangle of crags and eroded slopes, but the views north and west are more than reward for the effort. Staffa, the Treshnish Isles, Inch Kenneth and Ulva all stand out like jewels, more so in the setting sun.

A good return route is to take a slightly lower line below Creag nam

En route Beinn na Sreine showing the Isle of Inchkenneth

Fitheach, following a route roughly parallel with the Creag a' Ghaill cliffs. This crosses some unavoidable tussocky and probably boggy terrain before crossing several small streams. Before the rise up to the final high ground you will need to stay above the steep cliff edge on your left. Finally, reach the line of the outward ascent and return to your starting point.

16. BEINN A'GHRAIG DEER HERD HILL (591M/1,939FT)

MAP	OS SHEET 47&48 (GR 541373)
DISTANCE	9KM
ASCENT	600M
TIME	3–4.5 HRS
ACCESS	KNOCK (GR 545388) (FOR MULL ACCESS SEE END OF MULL ROUTES)
DIFFICULTY	FAIRLY STEEP ASCENT AND PATHLESS, WITH CRAGS IN THE UPPER REACHES
SUMMARY	A steep-sided and rocky satellite top of Ben More with a fine, narrow summit ridge. Beinn a'Ghraig has immense character.

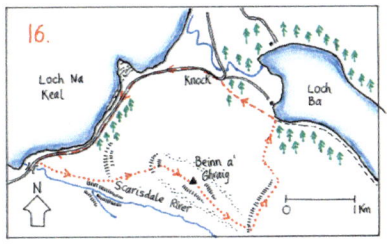

BEINN A'GHRAIG IS the most northerly of Ben More's attendant tops and could be climbed as a starter for the bigger feast of these tops, culminating in the Munro of Ben More. However, the described route is a short, circular traverse of the hill, finishing with a walk along the southern shore of Loch Bà.

There is limited parking at the start of the Loch Bà track at Knock. The first part of the route follows the coast road for 3km to the foot of the Scarisdale River from where the ascent begins. If you prefer to do this road walk at the end of the trip, then park at Scarisdale.

Stay left of the river gorge initially, keeping right of a rock terrace higher up. The angle steepens considerably to another band of crags which can be tackled directly by numerous gullies and grassy rakes. Alternatively, veer right to gain the summit ridge by scree.

From the western top, descend slightly before climbing quartzite slabs and grass to reach the main summit, a grand, airy viewpoint feeling like a

Beinn a'Ghraig from the north

Ben More from Beinn a'Ghraig

much higher hill. Take time to enjoy the extensive views in all directions.

Continue along the ridge, negotiating one slightly awkward rocky descent to reach a stony col. Beyond is a curious quartzite natural wall crossing the ridge and is the remains of the volcanic Loch Bà ring dyke, stretching right down to the loch itself. This interesting geo-logical feature makes an ideal line of descent. Gain the top of the wall by an optional scramble, or take any number of easier routes.

Follow the edge of the dyke down to a stream on intermittent rock slabs and scree, before following the stream down grassy slopes and finally through trees to the track on the south shore of Loch Bà. A kilometre of pleasant walking takes you back to your starting point at Knock.

17. BEINN NA DUATHARACH HILL OF DARKNESS (456M/1,495FT)

MAP	OS SHEET 49 (GR 604363)
DISTANCE	14KM
ASCENT	460M
TIME	4–6 HRS
ACCESS	PENNYGOWN (A849)
DIFFICULTY	LEVEL VEHICLE TRACK FOLLOWED BY PATHLESS, GRASSY ASCENT
SUMMARY	Occupying a central position in Mull's main hill massif, Beinn na Duatharach is a superlative viewpoint with real character.

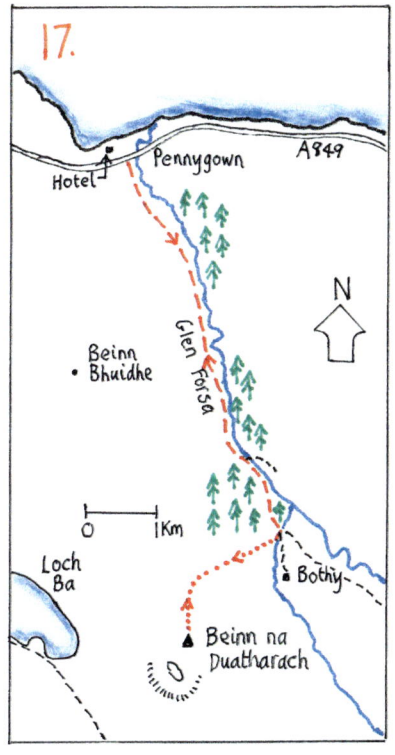

LYING IN THE shadow of its more illustrious neighbour of Beinn Talaidh to the southeast, Beinn na Duatharach is, nevertheless, an overlooked gem of a hill with steep approaches from all directions. Its summit cone is guarded by terraces of crags and the hill has undeniable charm and individuality.

The easiest approach to the hill is via Glen Forsa to the north, the start at Pennygown being annoyingly on OS Sheet 48. The entrance to Glen Forsa is at a tiny dual carriageway section of the A849, where parking may be problematic. There is a very small parking place just west of the entrance, but it would be more sensible to use the parking area outside the Glen Forsa Hotel, a few hundred metres west, on the north side of the road – provided you use the bar facilities after your walk – not a profound hardship!

A bike would be useful for the initial 5km stretch along the Glen Forsa track,

Beinn na Duatharach from the north

being an easy, flat approach route offering a fine view of the prominent Beinn Talaidh ridge in the distance. Note that a herd of cows often roam freely onto the track so take care, especially with dogs around. The track gradually approaches the River Forsa on the left, passing a new fishing lodge. Ignore a left fork crossing a bridge and continue until the track turns southward at a gap in the forestry.

Around here you will see the obvious grassy ridge leading up to Beinn na Duatharach and on the left, the twin ridges of Beinn Bheag and Beinn Talaidh. Nestling serenely on the lower slopes is the MBA-maintained bothy of Tomsleibhe (mountain knoll), an excel-

lent twin-roomed stone cottage offering rough accommodation and a good base for exploration.

The eagle-eyed will spot what looks like a giant pair of antlers at a track junction just to the left. Closer inspection, however, reveals it to be the mangled propeller of a Dakota aircraft which crashed into the slopes of Beinn Talaidh in February 1945. Miraculously, most of the crew survived the crash and one who saw a light burning in a shepherd's cottage, managed to reach it and gain help. The propeller was erected as a monument and stands at the junction of the Glen Forsa and Tomsleibhe tracks.

At the bend in the track before the

Loch Ba from Beinn na Duatharach

monument, leave the track and take to the lower slopes of Beinn Duatharach on sketchy sheep furrows and ATV tracks. Eventually, after steeper grass climbing, reach a flattish area with a wee lochan. Just beyond is the final craggy cone of the hill. A grassy right to left sloping terrace forms a convenient ascent route to the summit cairn, perched on a rocky plinth. The best view looks north-west along the expanse of Loch Bà. A tangled arc of mountains dominates the remaining views.

Return by the outward route. If transport is not a problem, it would be a fine expedition to descend into Glen Cannel and follow the track out on the west side of Loch Bà to Knock, at the head of Loch Keal.

18. SPEINNE MÒR BIG PARTITION (444M/1,458FT)

MAP	OS SHEET 47 (GR 499498)
DISTANCE	10KM
ASCENT	300M
TIME	3–4 HRS
ACCESS	WESTERN END OF MISHNISH LOCHS (GR 465524)
DIFFICULTY	ROUGH PATH AND BOGGY IN PLACES. GOOD RETURN TRACK
SUMMARY	The highest hill in north Mull provides a grand, high-level walk with excellent views.

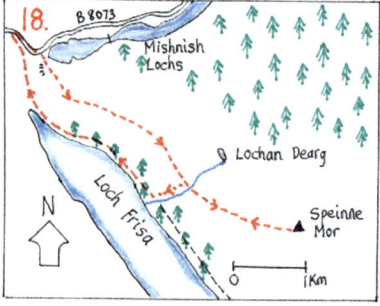

SPEINNE MÒR IS the highest point of the long whaleback ridge, lying to the north of the longest and largest freshwater loch on Mull, Loch Frisa. It may not possess a craggy, pointed profile, or be particularly prominent, but its summit panorama is extensive, and it is second only to Ben More in terms of popularity, particularly with locals.

The hill could easily be combined with 'S Àirde Beinn (see following route) in a back-to-back trip, as the starting point for this hill is only 1km away from the start of the route about to be outlined.

Park just west of the highest point on the Tobermory to Dervaig road, where there is a small quarry on the left with a gate at its rear. There is room for about three or four cars. Go through the gate and follow the grassy path up a series of steep inclines, with a glorious view east to the Mishnish lochs. The top loch, Carnain an Amais (the meeting cairn loch), takes its name from funeral cairns marking resting places for the coffin bearers en route to the burial ground at Dervaig.

Higher up, the path avoids the ridge crest and keeps to the right, giving fine views along the length of Loch Frisa. Some gravelly peat banks offer drier and firmer ground in between the boggier sections. For much of the route you are following the line of an old fence, just a few metres to the right, a good aid in misty conditions.

Tobermory and Beinn Hiant from Speinne Mor

Descend slightly, through a decidedly boggy section, to cross the outflow stream of Lochan Dearg, a small hill lochan which will not be noticed until you gain height. A steep section then follows before the fence is finally abandoned and the path continues on over a frustrating series of false summits, to eventually arrive at the summit trig point surrounded by a ring cairn. This is similar to Ben More's summit, only its trig point is long since gone.

The summit panorama rivals that of Ben More and the view north to Tobermory, backed by graceful Ben Hiant in Ardnamurchan is simply breathtaking. To the south, the whole of Mull's main mountain group fills the horizon.

To vary the return, retrace the ridge to the boggy col below the summit and cross the outflow of Lochan Dearg. Descend to the left, beyond a craggy section, through heather and bracken and a felled forestry area. This leads to the vehicle track skirting the north shore of Loch Frisa. Turn right and follow the track for 2.5km to reach the road. Turn right uphill and reach your car in only half a kilometre.

19. 'S ÀIRDE BEINN HIGHEST HILL (295M/968FT)

MAP	OS SHEET 47 (GR 471537)
DISTANCE	3KM
ASCENT	160M
TIME	1–1.5 HRS
ACCESS	B8073 ROAD (GR 475527)
DIFFICULTY	INITIAL EASY BUT BOGGY PATH, FOLLOWED BY A PLEASANT CIRCULAR RIDGE
SUMMARY	The curious hill of 'S Àirde Beinn provides an ideal short summer evening's walk giving maximum reward for minimum effort with its panoramic summit views. It could easily be combined with the previous route.

THE DOLERITE, VOLCANIC plug of 'S Àirde Beinn is not high by any standard, despite its odd name, but it is the highest point, north of the Tobermory–Dervaig road, affording it superb all round views. It is the largest and best-known example of a Tertiary volcanic plug in western Scotland.

If driving from Tobermory, the starting point is at a ruined cottage on the right, opposite the Mishnish lochs. There is a small two-car parking spot just before the ruin. If this is full, go back about a quarter of a kilometre and park at a large quarry.

Just beyond the ruin, go through a gate and follow a very rough and often boggy path up the vegetated hillside. In summer, these slopes are ablaze with bright yellow bog asphodel and the song of skylarks high above is a

The 'crater loch' on 'S Àirde Beinn

delightful musical accompaniment. The craggy south summit of the hill is visible for most of this initial daunder. At a fork in the path, take the left branch, which climbs more steeply up to your first view of what is commonly known as 'Crater Loch'. This is a beautiful, secluded wee lochan, nestling in a hollow, surrounded by a 'crater rim'. Despite the name, it is not actually a crater but was formed during the last ice age.

Climb up to the south summit to gain an appreciation of this secretive, placid body of water completely surrounded by a craggy mountain ridge – a marvellous spot. The highest point is about halfway along the western rim and is visited first if doing a clockwise circuit. The best view, however, is from the cairn at the northern end of the loch, which is marked 292m on the OS map.

As well as offering wide-ranging views of Mull itself, the view east to Ardnamurchan is very fine, with Ben Hiant (a Hugh) looking resplendent in evening sunshine.

Complete the rim circuit and descend by the path, following an old stone wall and the stream outflow from the loch. This joins the ascent path at the junction mentioned earlier.

GETTING TO MULL

Vehicle ferry from Oban to Craignure. Booking advised. • Vehicle ferry from Lochaline to Fishnish. No booking required. Only 20 minutes. • Vehicle ferry from Kilchoan (Ardnamurchan) to Tobermory. No booking required. Tel: 08000 66 5000 for all ferry information.

IONA

20. DUN I (IONA FORT) (101M/331FT)

MAP	OS SHEET 48 (GR 284252)
DISTANCE	3KM
ASCENT	101M
TIME	1–2 HRS
ACCESS	THE JETTY, IONA (SEE BELOW FOR ACCESS TO IONA)
DIFFICULTY	PROBABLY THE EASIEST ASCENT IN THIS BOOK!
SUMMARY	Dun I, the highest point of Iona, has arguably the finest view from any hill of comparable height in Scotland. The phrase 'maximum reward from minimal effort' could have been coined for this grand wee eminence.

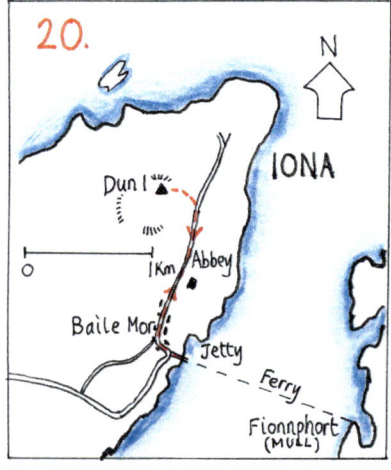

IONA'S UNIQUE COMBINATION of ancient gnarled gneiss, white shell-sand beaches, subtle hues, sparkle and purity of light and deeply ingrained Christian history, give it a magical essence not found anywhere else.

Although the route to be described is a 'there and back' visit to the hill, the keen walker will no doubt wish to combine the ascent with a visit to many of the fine beaches. Iona is an island perfect for individual exploration.

From the ferry jetty, walk directly up the road past some cottages, turning right past the ruins of a nunnery. This leads, in half a kilometre, to Iona Abbey, which can be visited now or later. Continue along the road past some houses on the left, where there is a signpost for Dun I to the left of the road. Go through the gate and follow the path across a field to the craggy eastern slopes of the hill. A path of sorts swings round to the left and meanders its way up to the summit, where there is a large cairn and trig point.

Dun I cairn

The northern aspect is a vertical rock wall, so care is needed on the summit. With the whole of Iona spread around in verdant green, lined by pure, white beaches and Staffa, the Treshnish Isles and the Wilderness coastline of Mull all vying for attention, it will be difficult to draw yourself away from this sacred spot.

Return the same way, or take time to explore the wonderful beaches on the north and east of the island.

GETTING TO IONA

Frequent passenger ferry from Fhionnphort on Mull, taking 10 minutes. Operates summer only and other times by request. No cars allowed. (Tel: 01680 812343).

ULVA

21. BEINN CHREAGACH (ROCKY HILL) (313M/1,026FT)

MAP	OS SHEET 47 (GR 403402)
DISTANCE	13KM
ASCENT	420M
TIME	4–5 HRS
ACCESS	THE JETTY, ULVA (SEE BELOW FOR ACCESS TO ULVA)
DIFFICULTY	GOOD APPROACH AND RETURN PATHS; TRACKLESS HEATHER ON THE HILL ITSELF
SUMMARY	Ulva's high point has a remote and wild ambience, and has stupendous views.

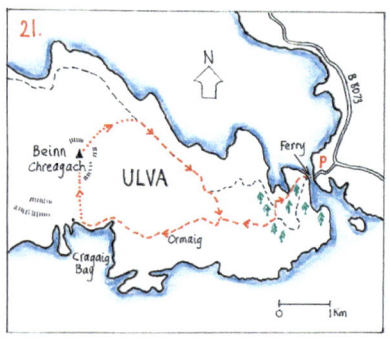

ULVA IS SEPARATED from Mull by a narrow channel, only 150m wide, yet this quiet backwater seems a world apart from the hustle and bustle of contemporary life. The name's origin is likely Old Norse for 'Wolf Isle', though the Gaelic 'Ullamh dha' (ready for occupation) is also a possibility.

The island has had a notable history, being the birthplace of Lachlan Macquarie (the 'Father of Australia'), David Livingstone's father in 1788 and having borne the brunt of the most savage and cruel Clearances from 1846 to 1851. Recently, Ulva has again been in the news for the controversial buy-out by the current residents with help from the Scottish government.

The described route is a clockwise circuit, passing the Clearance settlements of Ormaig and Cragaig, before ascending the hill and returning by the main vehicle track to the north.

From the jetty and boathouse, follow the track off to the right round a sharp bend and continue on to a junction. Go left here and follow the track to a building on the right, where a sharp turn right takes you uphill through a pleasant wooded area and onto open, bracken-covered heath. Further on, look out for a smaller footpath going off to the left, indicated by a signpost.

Ben More from Beinn Chreagach

Take this path, which eventually descends to the ruined shielings of Ormaig and Cragaig, set in swathes of grassy swards and bracken. There is a little ruined water mill where the path crosses the stream in Glen Glass.

The path ends at the idyllic, sheltered haven of Cragaig Bay, where there is a private bothy and standing stones. This beautiful spot holds special memories for me, as I spent my 50th birthday here at the bothy, with several others, whilst supervising a Kilgraston School Gold Duke of Edinburgh expedition. Relaxing outside the bothy, on a sunny, midgeless, late April evening, with a glass of red wine, gazing out to sparkling seas and islets, holds cherished memories.

Begin the ascent of Beinn Chreagach from here, where the vague south ridge of the hill rises up steeply through heather and bracken. Much of the stepped basalt terracing, a feature of Ulva, is conspicuous by its absence on this ascent, but is prevalent to the west. After about 40 minutes, arrive at the summit trig point and enjoy glorious views across Loch na Keal to Ben More and its attendant tops. This is a wonderful place to while away a good half hour.

To complete a grand circuit, wend your way down in a rough north-eastern direction, taking care to avoid the odd terraced crags and reach the stony vehicle track skirting the north side of the island. Turn right, and follow the track back to the jetty, partly by the outward route. Alternatively, take a footpath at GR 427396, which winds its way downhill to a track and old church. Turning right, then left, brings you back to the start.

GETTING TO ULVA

The ferry works on a request system: to call the boat, slide the wooden slat to reveal the red marker. Crossings take 5 minutes, 9am to 5pm, Mon to Fri and Sundays in summer only. No Saturday service at any time. (Tel: 01688 500226).

TIREE

22. BEINN CEANN A' MHARA HILL AT THE HEAD OF THE SEA (103M/338FT)

MAP	OS SHEET 46 (GR 938410)
DISTANCE	6KM
ASCENT	120M
TIME	2–3 HRS
ACCESS	BALEPHUIL (GR 958404)
DIFFICULTY	EASY BEACH WALKING, ROCKY COASTLINE AND GRASSY MACHAIR
SUMMARY	A beautiful, varied walk to a wild and rugged peninsula, with fantastic western sea cliffs and glorious views.

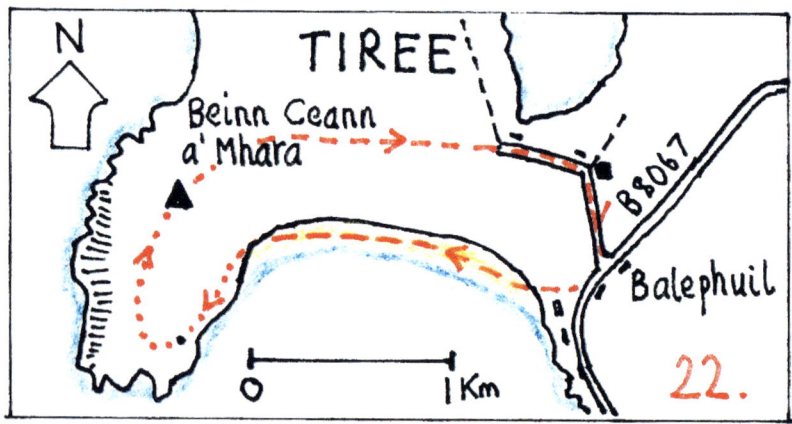

DESPITE TIREE BEING known for its flatness and superb white beaches, it also boasts three very distinct hills, all situated on the west of the island. Ironically, it is the lowest of these which is the most rugged and fully deserving of its 'Hugh' status. Its location, on the namesake headland on the extreme south-west corner of the island, gives it

a wild, romantic allure which is hard to resist and a delight to explore.

The best view of the hill is from Tràigh nan Gilean to the north and the shortest ascent would be from this beach. However, as the eastern beach of Tràigh Bhì is often described as the most picturesque beach on the island, the approach from Balephuil (at its

Beinn Ceann a' Mhara from the north (Tiree)

eastern end) is described here and is also conducive to an alternative return route across colourful machair.

Start in the tiny hamlet of Balephuil, with its telephone box and quaint houses. Walk directly over the grass, past some white cottages, to descend easily to the beautifully curving strand of Tràigh Bhì, with the craggy bulk of Beinn Ceann a' Mhara looming at the end. After reaching the end of the sands, it is worth following the coastline on grassy slopes, above the shoreline, for about half a kilometre, to reach the remains of St Patrick's Chapel, dating from the 7th century and containing two stones etched with crosses. A few hundred metres west of here is the site of an old fort, but little remains.

Climb directly upwards on grass, to follow the edge of precipitous drops on the left where, in the summer months, the cliffs are alive with sea birds. The summit of the hill consists of two dis-

Beinn Ceann a' Mhara from Balephuil

tinct tops, the southernmost one is the lower, but with a larger cairn perched on a crag, it is a marvellous spot to drink in the magnificent views of the bulk of Tiree. Drop down to a gap and easily ascend to the true summit of the hill and another excuse for a break and photography.

From the top, follow a fence south-east, to reach a corner, before taking a roughly easterly direction, over undulating terrain, eventually leading to excellent grass and wild flower machair, interspersed with dunes. Follow a faint, grassy path to a large shed and cattle grid, from where a track leads to a farm. Turn right here, to follow the road south, taking you back to Bale-phuil and the start of the route.

GETTING TO TIREE

Tiree is normally reached by Caledonian MacBrayne Ferries (CalMac) from Oban (www.calmac.co.uk) or by air from Glasgow and Oban (www.highlandairways.co.uk).

23. AN SGÙRR THE ROCKY PEAK (393M/1,290FT)

MAP	OS SHEET 39 (GR 463847)
DISTANCE	8KM
TIME	3–4H RS
ACCESS	THE PIER (SEE BELOW FOR ACCESS TO EIGG)
DIFFICULTY	DESPITE APPEARANCES, A FAIRLY STRAIGHTFORWARD WALK, MAINLY ON PATHS; OPTIONAL SCRAMBLING
SUMMARY	No visit to Eigg is complete without the ascent of this incredible wedge of rock, perhaps the most instantly recognisable of any island summit.

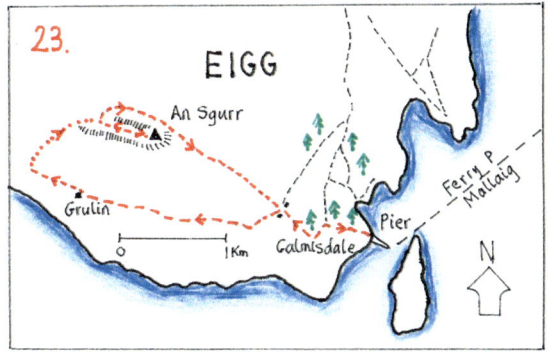

An Sgùrr, or the Sgùrr of Eigg as it also known, is the largest residual mass of columnar pitchstone lava in Britain, forming a craggy, 2km long ridge, ending abruptly in a sheer face at its eastern extremity. On first sight, the hill seems totally impregnable, but like Suilven in Assynt, there are chinks in its armour by which the walker can gain the summit ridge.

THE NAME 'EIGG' may be a derivation from the Norse 'egg', meaning 'edge', or from the Gaelic 'eag', for 'notch'.

After a long and sometimes troubled period of good, bad and indifferent landowners, history was made in 1997, when a plaque known as the Independence Stone was unveiled to commemorate the purchase of the island by its residents, a groundbreaking deal.

The outlined route is partly circular, ascending from the south and descending to the north of the summit ridge. Beginning at the pier in Galmisdale, take the uphill road past the Independence Stone and enter a woodland plantation. Follow the track, eventually

En route to Eigg and An Sgùrr

to a gate heading into an open field. Go through the gate, following a grassy track, where there is a magnificent view of the steep nose of An Sgùrr rising proudly above Galmisdale House.

The distinctive columnar formation of the cliffs is a result of fast cooling of the pitchstone lava, and An Sgùrr itself is a remnant of an ancient lava-filled valley resulting from volcanic eruptions on Rum, 50 million years ago. Glacial and post-glacial erosion have stripped the surrounding softer basalt to leave the hard ridge you see before you.

Beyond Galmisdale House, take a left fork along a track, running high above the shoreline across the heather moor. Look out for golden eagles, which are regularly spotted soaring above the high ridge to your right. In spring and early summer, the plaintive cry of the cuckoo can be heard, while kestrels, ravens and tiny wheatears should be in evidence.

In less than 2km from Galmisdale House, you will pass the isolated, white-washed cottage of Grulin, formerly a bothy, but now locked and privately owned. This point is the end of the main track, but continue to follow the coastline on an intermittent footpath for another half kilometre, before leaving the path to climb easy grass slopes to an obvious gap in the crags above.

After only 100m of ascent you will reach the knobbly ridge of An Sgùrr, peppered with several small lochans.

An Sgùrr

Turn right and follow the skyline over rough ground, keeping to the crest of the ridge. Optional rock scrambling opportunities are available on curious pitchstone formations for the more adventurous. Pick up a path on the crest and follow it to the triangulation pillar perched perilously close to the edge of a sheer drop.

Not surprisingly, the view from this airy vantage point is breathtaking. The islands of Muck, Coll, Tiree and Skye are all visible in clear weather, while the rugged spine of the Rum Cuillin dominate the northern outlook.

The return route is often used as an ascent route and retraces steps by backtracking along the ridge for about half a kilometre, then descending to the right by a small cairn. A natural gully leads downwards on a reasonably clear path, which then follows the base of the northern escarpment and nose, before crossing open moorland to Galmisdale House and the outward track.

GETTING TO EIGG

CalMac passenger ferry from Mallaig every day except Wednesday in summer (Tel: 01687 462403). • Arisaig Marine run ferries to Eigg from May to September on most days (Tel: 01687 450224). • There is no hotel on Eigg, but there are self-catering cottages, B&Bs and guesthouses. • See the island's website: www.isleofeigg.net.

RUM

24. BLOODSTONE HILL (388M/1,273FT)
25. ORVAL (571M/1,873FT)

MAP	OS SHEET 39 (GR 315006, 334992)
DISTANCE	25KM
ASCENT	750M
TIME	9–11 HRS
ACCESS	KINLOCH (FOR ACCESS TO RUM, SEE END)
DIFFICULTY	A LONG AND DEMANDING EXPEDITION, THOUGH MAINLY ON TRACKS AND ROUGH PATHS WITH POTENTIALLY SERIOUS STREAM CROSSINGS
SUMMARY	This fine but challenging walk is a grand circuit of the two most prominent western hills of Rum. If staying at the remote bothy at Guirdil Bay, a circuit of Glen Guirdil is also briefly described, including the extra summit of Fionchra.

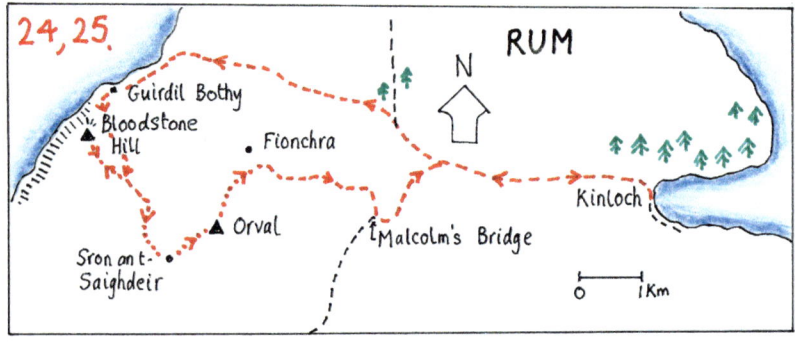

THE RUM CUILLIN traverse is undoubtedly the star attraction for most hillwalkers, but the more discerning visitor searching for isolation will find this overlooked part of the island a real wilderness experience. Ideally, for those with time at their disposal, a couple of nights spent at the wild and lonely Guirdil bothy would be the classic way to explore Rum's smaller hills.

Despite the name 'Bloodstone' conjuring up images of pirates and shipwrecks, the hill derives its name from a green rock (bloodstone), speckled with the red mineral, jasper, and used to be quarried to make jewellery. Orval, on the other hand, is *Oir Bhal*, a Gaelic/Norse fusion, meaning gold hill, which neatly extends the jewel theme. From a walker's point of view, these are certainly two gems awaiting discovery.

From the main settlement at Kinloch, follow the track north past Kinloch Castle, before turning left to head west through Kinloch Glen on an excellent Land Rover track. After 3.5km take the right fork, crossing the Kinloch River and then to another bridge over the Kilmory River. Just after crossing a stream, take a left fork near a woodland plantation. This is more of a pony path than a proper track and climbs gradually northwards above the trees, before heading west over a wide bealach into Glen Shellesder. This path is notoriously badly drained, even in dry weather and there are plenty of small burns to cross.

Descend gradually towards the wild west coast of Rum and turn left to make an unavoidable crossing of the Glen Shellesder Burn. In spate, this may present a serious challenge. From here, it is only 1km coastal walk to Guirdil, albeit with a final stream crossing about halfway.

Guirdil is a beautifully sheltered, tiny bay, backed by the protective, craggy bulk of Bloodstone Hill and bestowed with the human fingerprint of Guirdil bothy, all that remains of a once proud crofting community, other than a few ruins. If you are fully equipped with sleeping bag, food, stove – and whisky – then a few nights at Guirdil could just be the cure for all ills.

You will immediately notice that Bloodstone Hill is ringed with steep crags on its upper slopes and so a direct assault is not recommended. Of more immediate concern, however, is the crossing of Guirdil River, normally possible at its outflow near the sea but may require the removal of boots and socks. In real spate conditions, you may need to follow it inland until a suitable crossing point can be located.

Once across, follow the river uphill, on a track running parallel to a wooded enclosure on the right. Beyond the wood, make a rising traverse up the steep grass slopes forming the east flank of Bloodstone Hill. Cross two easy gullies and continue the rising traverse below crags to eventually reach an intermittent path leading to Bealach an Dubh-Bhraigh, the broad grassy saddle lying south of Bloodstone Hill. Just before the bealach, join a stalkers' path at a tiny lochan.

Turn right and follow the stalkers' path north-west, climbing steadily, before losing height slightly and then rising again to finally reach the slabby summit and small cairn. Sheer cliffs and steep craggy slopes guard the summit to the north and north-west and this eagles' eyrie gives stupendous views

Bloodstone Hill from Guirdil

across to Sanday and Canna; and on a clear day, to the Outer Isles and Skye – a magical spot.

Return to the small lochan at the bealach and continue along the path for about 300m before turning right to climb the obvious northern spur of Sron an t-Saighdeir, the western outlier of Orval. After a 270m ascent on tussocky grass and scree, reach the broad ridge, marked with a cairn.

Orval stands just over 1km to the east and is easily reached by following the broad ridge over two minor tops. The rounded summit of Orval is topped with a cairn and trig point and provides fine views of the Rum Cuillin to the south-east.

Continue north-east from Orval's summit, following the edge of its steep western flank. A final steep descent leads to the Bealach a' Bhraigh Bhig and rejoins the stalkers' path, which contours round the head of Glen Guirdil.

If you are staying at Guirdil bothy,

then an ideal circuit can be completed by climbing northwards for a few hundred metres and a 90m height gain, to reach the summit of Fionchra. This ascent takes only 15 minutes and could also be included as a 'there and back' from the bealach. Fionchra's north-west ridge leads directly down to the bothy, but a line of crags half way down will need to be avoided by dropping westwards into Glen Guirdil.

To continue to Kinloch, follow the stalkers' path downwards round a bend and into a wide, grassy corrie, passing a small lochan. This can be boggy in or after wet weather and the path crosses several streams before finally reaching the Land Rover track just east of Malcolm's Bridge.

Turn left and follow the track round a large bend to rejoin the original outward track in less than 2km. From here, it is 3.5km back to Kinloch.

GETTING TO RUM

CalMac offers a ferry service from Mallaig to Rum averaging five times a week. Please note cars are not allowed. See CalMac website for details. Accommodation on Rum ranges from wild camping and bothies through to a self-catering bunkhouse and a luxury guest house.

SKYE AND RASAAY – 25 HUGHS

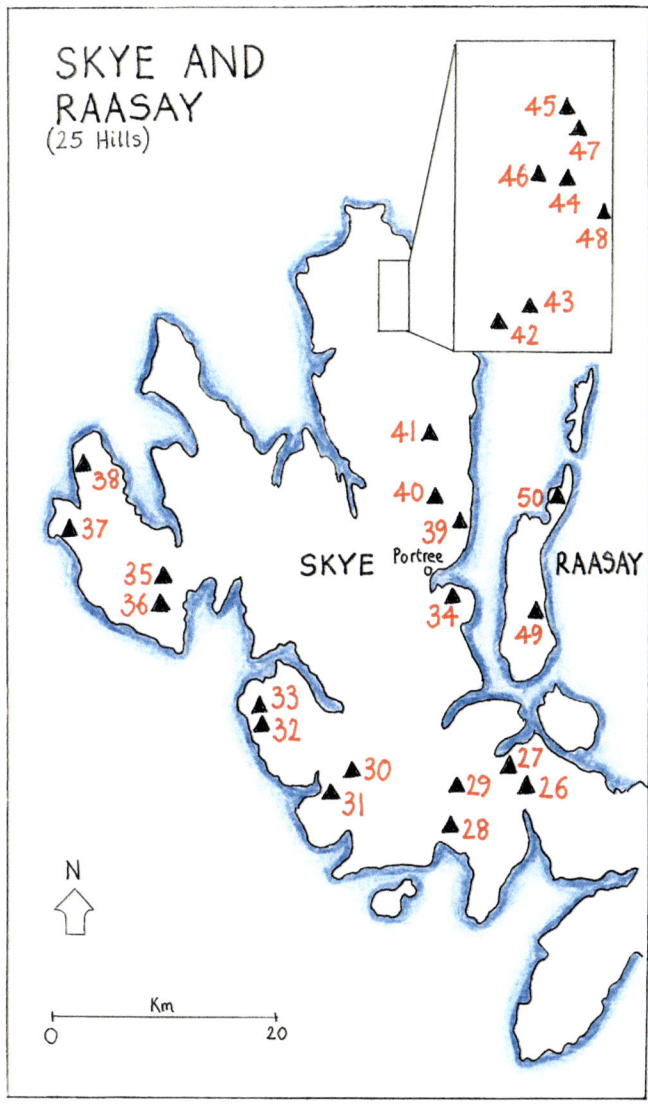

SKYE AND RASAAY
(25 Hills)

45

47

46

44

48

43

42

41

40

39

50

38

37

35

36

SKYE

Portree

RAASAY

34

49

33

32

30

31

27

29

26

28

N

Km

0   20

SKYE

26. BEINN NA CRO HILL OF THE FOLD (572M/1,878FT)
27. GLAS BHEINN MHÒR BIG GREY HILL (570M/1,870FT)

MAP	OS SHEET 32 (GR 569242, 553258)
DISTANCE	11KM
ASCENT	1,140M
TIME	4.5–6 HRS
ACCESS	HEAD OF LOCH SLAPIN
DIFFICULTY	EASY ASCENT ON BOTH HILLS, WITH VAGUE PATHS
SUMMARY	An ideal objective, when perhaps the higher hills and Cuillin are lost in cloud. Beinn na Cro is a superlative viewpoint for Clach Glas and Blà Bheinn.

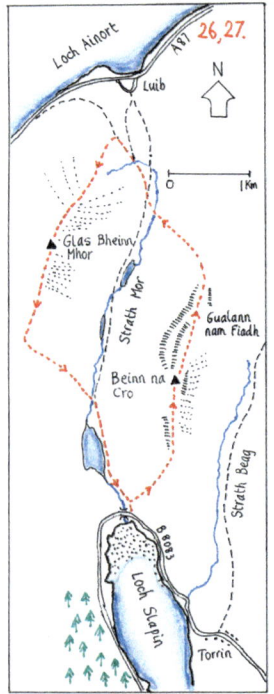

THESE TWO VERY prominent peaks are part of the Eastern Red Hills and are separated from each other by the deep trench of Strath Mor, where a public right of way runs from Loch Slapin to Luib, on Loch Ainort. Both hills have long, elongated ridges, aligned roughly north to south and provide excellent walking.

The described route is a circuit including both hills together, but for those wishing to climb the hills separately, it would be best to tackle Glas Bheinn Mhòr from Luib, to the north, returning by the right of way in Strath Mor. Climbing Beinn na Cro on its own is best effected by the described ascent, but returning by the Gualann nam Fiadh col and the right of way path in Strath Beag.

The public right of way through Strath Mor begins just east of the bridge at the head of Loch Slapin, where there is limited parking. Walk up the track for about 100m, before branching off on a very rough path to the right, just beyond a fence. This meanders up to the left of an obvious depression. Pockets of

Beinn na Cro and Glas Bheinn Mhòr from Loch Slapin

Raasay from Beinn na Cro summit

smooth, pinkish, granite blocks are an aid to ascent in dry conditions but can be lethally slippery when wet. Further up, the ridge becomes more pronounced, and the angle gradually eases, with a distinct change from granite to basalt in the upper reaches.

The airy summit is topped by a wee cairn and is a marvellous vantage point for the whole castellated Clach Glas–Blà Bheinn ridge to the south-west. The celebrated landscape photographer, Colin Prior, spent many hours on the slopes of this hill in order to capture

Loch Slapin from Glas Bheinn Mhor

perfect winter conditions on this classic mountain ridge (my own favourite Scottish ridge). There is also a fine view north over Loch Ainort, to the island of Raasay, with its distinctive high point of Dùn Caan (a Hugh).

Descend the mainly easy-angled north ridge, taking care on the odd steeper section. If omitting Glas Bheinn Mhòr, descend easy grass slopes right to Gualann nam Fiadh (shoulder of the deer) and drop down to the Strath Beag path, which exits at Torrin, 2km south along the road from the starting point.

To continue to Glas Bheinn Mhòr, stay on the north ridge until steep crags force you left. Continue to head north, before gradually swinging west to cross the stream and reach the path on the opposite side. Follow this north for a short distance, taking a left fork, which makes a rising traverse. After half a kilometre, cut off left to make a beeline for the hill's north ridge, where an old stone wall can be followed all the way to the summit. You will notice that this hill is composed of a different type of granite, being greyish in colour (hence the hill name), unlike the pinkish hues of the main Red Hills to the east.

Follow the old wall down the pleasant south ridge to the wide bealach below Belig, before descending grassy slopes east to Strath Mor. In wet conditions, the river in Strath Mor may be tricky to cross, in order to reach the path. If in doubt, walk out to the road on the west side of the river to your starting point.

28. SGÙRR NA STRÌ PEAK OF STRIFE (497M/1,631FT)

MAP	OS SHEET 32 (GR 499193)
DISTANCE	17KM
ASCENT	730M
TIME	6–8 HRS
ACCESS	START OF CAMASUNARY ACCESS TRACK (GR 545173)
DIFFICULTY	EASY APPROACH TRACK, FOLLOWED BY A RIVER CROSSING AND VAGUE PATH, BECOMING MORE WELL DEFINED HIGHER UP; THE ROUTE INVOLVES THE CROSSING OF THE 'BAD STEP' (A SCRAMBLE), BUT CAN BE AVOIDED BY RETURNING THE SAME WAY
SUMMARY	This hill packs a punch like few others. Bold, rocky, striking, with grandstand views of the whole Cuillin ridge, Sgùrr na Strì must lay claim to being one of the finest, if not *the* finest wee hill in Scotland.

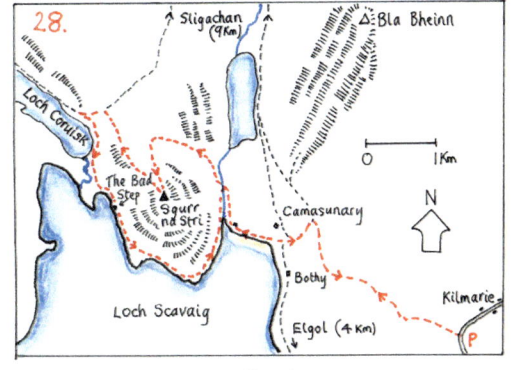

THE BLUNT, GABBRO profile of Sgùrr na Strì rises directly from the shores of Loch Scavaig in soaring crags, gullies and buttresses, to a twin-topped summit, split by a fissure, which almost divides this miniature mountain in two. For the armchair tourist, it remains shy and reclusive, unless seen from the jetty at Elgol, on the Strathaird peninsula, where its twin south facing buttresses, split by the aforementioned fissure, give it an air of height, presence and impregnability almost upstaging the main Cuillin ridge behind.

The mountain is an effective barrier between the idyllic bay at Camasunary and the jewel in the Cuillin crown, Loch Coruisk. Having spent regular holidays at Camasunary Lodge since the early 1990s, I have ascended Sgùrr na Strì on countless occasions by countless routes in summer and winter and never tire

Sgurr na Strì from Elgol

of its magic and charm. The explosive view from the summit on a clear day never fails to arrest and reel the senses. I would easily rank the hill as one of my favourites in Scotland.

The described route is the easiest line of ascent, from the closest approach route near the village of Kilmarie. It returns by the coastal path, crossing the infamous 'Bad Step', to give a partly circular route. If scrambling is not in your remit, then return by the ascent route. Longer approaches are possible from the likes of Elgol and even Sligachan. There is a new bothy at Camasunary for those who may wish to make a weekend of the outing.

The start of the route is at the large lay-by opposite the start of the rough gravel Land Rover track leading to Camasunary. This is about 4.5km short of Elgol, on the Broadford to Elgol road. Follow the track as it meanders its way slightly uphill then downwards to cross a stream before climbing in a series of zigzags to its high point at Am Mam (the pass) at around 160m of height. The track was constructed by Army engineers in the 1960s to improve access to Loch Coruisk, and there were even plans to remove the Bad Step using explosives – thankfully this mad, latter idea did not materialise!

As you round a bend beyond Am Mam, the first glimpse of the Cuillin ridge is simply breathtaking – from the

Sgurr na Strì

prominent nose of Garbh-bheinn on the left, to the pinnacle ridge of Sgùrr nan Gillean and the soaring south ridge of Blà Bheinn on the right. Standing centre-stage is the imposing bastion of Sgùrr na Strì, the ascent route heading initially into the corrie on its right.

Slightly further on, the whole bay of Camasunary reveals itself: a gentle sward of green machair and white sandy beach, with its two white buildings. Camasunary literally means 'bay of the white shieling'. The small white building furthest away is the old bothy which, at the time of writing, is being renovated as a private summer residence of the owner of the larger lodge house in the foreground. The new bothy is the stone building way off to the left and maintained by the MBA.

Descend, via a hairpin bend and head for the old bothy, either along the beach, or by a grassy path above the beach. Beyond the old bothy is a fairly substantial river, where you will no doubt spot the remains of old stanchions, which used to support a pedestrian suspension bridge, swept away in the early 1980s. I can remember crossing this bridge in 1979, when its days were numbered.

Various sets of steppingstones now aid the walker across the river, the best being at a small island in the river, several hundred metres further upstream. As a last resort, removing boots and

Sgurr na Strì and Camasunary

socks may be the only viable option.

Once safely across, turn right and make a gradual, rising traverse into the corrie between Sgùrr na Strì and the imposing cliffs of Sgùrr Hain to your right. A path of sorts weaves its way into the upper reaches of the corrie. If in doubt, head for the left of two obvious bealachs, which are separated by a rocky skyline hillock.

Higher up, weave through huge slabs and crags of gabbro, where the path becomes much more defined. The path approaches the bealach, before traversing off to the left to meet the north ridge of Sgùrr na Strì and the final leg to the summit. This ridge is complex and rocky, split by the fissure mentioned earlier, but the path upwards is initially very obvious, keeping well to the left of the actual ridge crest. More adventurous souls may wish to move right and scramble upwards on excellent, easy-angled slabs.

You will soon be forced into the central fissure, where a spot of rock clambering eventually leads to the obvious gap between the twin summits of the mountain. Climbing up to the left on a stony path takes you to the east summit, which has a grand, bird's-eye view of Camasunary Bay far below. For some people, the east summit is the pinnacle of their achievement and fail to venture onto the west top – don't be one of them! Despite the west summit

On the Bad Step

being slightly more difficult to reach, the views are truly magnificent.

Retrace steps to the central fissure and climb up the opposite side on another stony path, with one awkward step, to reach the small cairn perched on a slab. You will now witness what has been described as the finest view of the Cuillin. I would have no hesitation in declaring this to be the finest view from any Scottish mountain (see the picture at the start of the Introduction). Far below, the glittering waters of Loch Coruisk eat into the wild heart of the Cuillin, which rise majestically above in intricate acres of sublime rock architecture to an immutable, crenellated crest.

The Cuillin so dominate the view that one almost forgets the seaward views to Soay, backed by mountainous Rum and Eigg to its left. Sgùrr na Strì must be the only mountain where you get two summits, and crucially, two different views, for the price of one.

Rather than return by the ascent route, the described route descends the full length of the north ridge to Loch Coruisk and follows the coast path back to Camasunary via the Bad Step. Staying on the Coruisk side of the ridge enables much of the descent to be made on rough, easy-angled gabbro slabs, interspersed with grassy slopes and gullies. After about 1.5km you will reach a rough path which is followed round and down to Loch Coruisk itself.

Take time to savour the majesty of this unique mountain amphitheatre, before following the path through a natural cleft, to reach the sheltered cove of Loch nan Leachd (loch of the tomb), known locally as Scots' Cove. The coastal path here becomes hemmed in with large boulders, until you reach the obvious rock slab of the Bad Step. Climb up onto a prominent ledge and follow a natural shelf, using your hands to maintain balance on the slab above. The only awkward move is at the end of the shelf, where you drop down to a wide platform with an overhanging rock above. This all sounds horrendous but is not that difficult!

Beyond the 'not so bad step', the path rises and falls, passing through another natural cleft to leave the coast for a short distance. The final stretch, round the Rubha Ban leads back to Camasunary, where you re-cross the river and retrace steps back out to the road by the Land Rover track.

29. RUADH STAC RED STACK (493M/1,619FT)

MAP	OS SHEET 32 (GR 514233)
DISTANCE	10KM
ASCENT	470M
TIME	3–5 HRS
ACCESS	LAY-BY ABOVE LOCH AINORT ON A87 (GR 534267)
DIFFICULTY	INDISTINCT AND OFTEN BOGGY PATHS, PLUS SCREE AND LOOSE TERRAIN
SUMMARY	This isolated, but bold little hill stands between the Graham of Marsco and Corbett of Garbh-bheinn. Despite its lower stature it offers panoramic views of the whole Cuillin ridge.

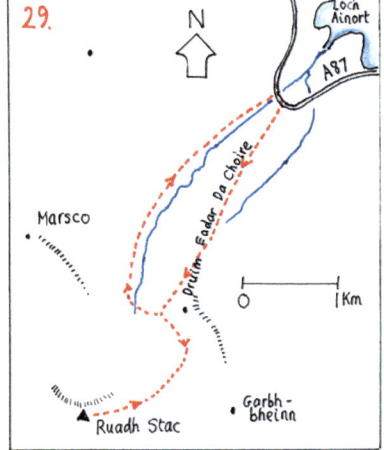

RUADH STAC'S STAR rating is undoubtedly for the stunning view it provides, not only of the Cuillin ridge, but its intimate view of the rarely seen north-western buttresses and gullies of Blà Bheinn. I have ascended this hill on numerous occasions from Camasunary

Lodge to the south and indeed, if you are based in the bothy at Camasunary, Ruadh Stac provides an ideal half day or summer evening's outing. Ideally, the hill could be included with an ascent of Marsco or Garbh-bheinn from the head of Loch Ainort. The described route is a 'Ruadh Stac only' option from Loch Ainort.

Park at the large lay-by on the A87, just north of the bend in the road. This lay-by is often used by bus parties to photograph the waterfall on the Allt Coire nam Bruadaran, so may be busy. Walk down the road and leave it just beyond the stream to gain the foot of the broad ridge named Druim Eadar Da Choire on the map. A vague path follows the crest of the ridge, which you follow for 2km, before contouring off to the right (bypassing the ridge summit) to reach a broad 323m col

Ruadh Stac from Blaven (the hill on the lower right)

between Marsco and Druim Eadar Da Choire. At this point there is a fine view of the steep and rocky north face of Ruadh Stac.

Your next aim is to reach the col between Ruadh Stac and Garbh-bheinn, which involves contouring round the bowl of Am Fraoch-choire (the heather corrie). Luckily, a path helps negotiate the sometimes-loose scree. Cross the head of a stream by a shallow gully, before slightly easier terrain leads to the col below Ruadh Stac. Ascend the broad east ridge on granite slabs, rock and scree to reach the flat, grassy summit.

Hopefully, if you haven't left this hill for a dreich day, you can appreciate the panoramic sweep of the saw-tooth Cuillin and the view south down Glen Sligachan to Camasunary and the sea.

To return, retrace steps to the first col encountered on the ascent. Either continue to retrace steps, or drop down the Coire nam Bruadaran to follow the left (west) bank of the burn on an intermittent, but often boggy path. This leads in less than 3km to the road and lay-by.

The author on Ruadh Stac
(Photo: Vicky Sherwood)

30. BEINN A' BHRAGHAD HILL OF THE NECK (461M/1,512FT)
31. AN CRUACHAN THE SMALL STACK OR CONICAL HILL (435M/1,428FT)

MAP	OS SHEET 32 (GR 410254, 382225)
DISTANCE	18KM
ASCENT	800M
TIME	6–8 HRS
ACCESS	GLEN EYNORT
DIFFICULTY	GOOD FORESTRY TRACKS ON APPROACH AND RETURN; PATHLESS, TUSSOCKY TERRAIN OTHERWISE
SUMMARY	These two little-frequented hills on the west side of Glen Brittle are marvellous viewpoints of the Cuillin, and An Cruachan in particular is a fine, graceful peak with a steep and craggy north face.

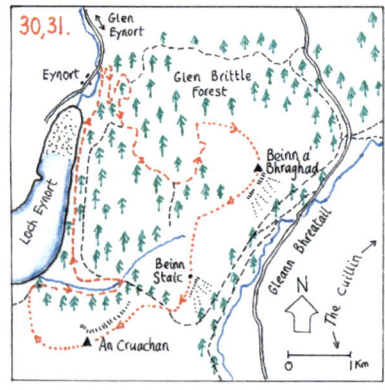

THE EARLY 20TH century Cuillin pioneer, Ben Humble, once said of the wee hills bordering the west side of Glen Brittle, that they are 'just about the finest viewpoint for the Cuillin'. I would guess that the rider 'just about' gives credence to Sgùrr na Strì, on the opposite side of the Cuillin (see Route 28).

The traverse of these hills, including the smaller, central peak of Beinn Staic, would at first sight seem to be best tackled from Glen Brittle and that indeed would be a quicker option than the route to be described. This, more natural round, begins at Glen Eynort and, crucially, does not involve brutally steep ascents or descents, as the Glen Brittle approach would entail. If climbing the two hills separately, then the Glen Brittle approach would probably hold favour. Beinn a' Bhraghad and Beinn Staic are both completely surrounded by Sitka spruce plantations, but the approach makes good use of forestry tracks.

Drive down the narrow Glen Eynort

road and park just past a cattle grid on the left, before the bridge over the Eynort river. Walk down the track to the left, with a sign indicating 'Glen Brittle circular', past a cottage on the left (Raven Cottage). Enter the forestry area, where you will see an information sign at a junction. Turn left here and follow the track via three hairpin bends to an upper track, which contours round Beinn a' Bhraghad and Beinn Staic.

Beinn Stac and An Cruachan from Beinn a' Bhraghad

There are two options at this point. The first is to turn right for about 1km, before turning left up to the vicinity of Bealach Eadar da Bheinn. A long loop left leads to a clearing and the end of the track. Heading east from here, on tussocky heather and the odd tree leads to open heath and the summit of Beinn a' Bhraghad. This was the route I used, but the second option would be to turn left and follow the track round to the north of the hill, before ascending via an obvious wide firebreak beginning at GR 407273. The second option would probably be marginally quicker.

The trig point on the hill is not actually the true summit, which lies several hundred metres to the south-west, across a rather flat, marshy area. Moving slightly east gives the finest view of the northern half of the Cuillin ridge, especially into Coire na Creiche, with its now curiously infamous 'Fairy Pools', a tourist magnet. On return to the car, I met an Italian couple who were looking for the Fairy Pools – I had to tell them they were in the wrong glen!

The shapely lines of An Cruachan look well from here, some 4km to the south-west, across the intermediate summit of Beinn Staic, your next objective. Descend the south-west ridge, with steep drops on your left, to Glen Brittle far below. Approaching the bealach, the going underfoot is awkward, over tree planting furrows and it is only near the summit of Beinn Staic that the terrain becomes significantly easier.

From Beinn Staic, descend quite steeply to the treeline and use a firebreak to reach the 'circular' track at Bealach Brittle. Turn right for about 50m before going left on a vague path to reach a gate and a rough track at the base of An Cruachan. Turn right here and follow this track until it peters out at the foot of the spur, named Guala a' Choire Mhòir (shoulder of the big corrie). This shoulder makes an ideal line of ascent along its crest, with steep,

The Cuillin from An Cruachan

craggy slopes falling away into the corrie on the right.

A final steepening leads to the summit trig point, perched on a rocky outcrop. This is another marvellous viewpoint, sitting majestically, directly above Loch Eynort, offering fine, seaward vistas, especially to the island of Rum.

Descend easy grass slopes in a north-west direction, to eventually reach an old farm track near Kraiknish, south of Loch Eynort. Before recent tree felling, it was possible to follow an old path along the shoreline, linking up with a forestry track. Unfortunately, now you will need to make a lengthy dogleg east, to cross the Allt Dabhoch, before doubling back on the circular forest route. This leads directly back to the starting point.

For those pushed for time, it would make sense to descend from this last hill by the ascent route and pick up the circular track at Bealach Brittle.

32. PRESHAL BEG LITTLE PRECIOUS (347M/1,138FT)
33. PRESHAL MORE BIG PRECIOUS (322M/1,056FT)

MAP	OS SHEET 32 (GR 329278, 333300)
DISTANCE	10KM
ASCENT	450M
TIME	4.5–6 HRS
ACCESS	TALISKER
DIFFICULTY	CROSS-COUNTRY ON MAINLY EASY, GRASSY TERRAIN.
SUMMARY	The round of this pair of strikingly individual little gems, may not be on any list of popular Skye walks, but once visited, you will wonder why.

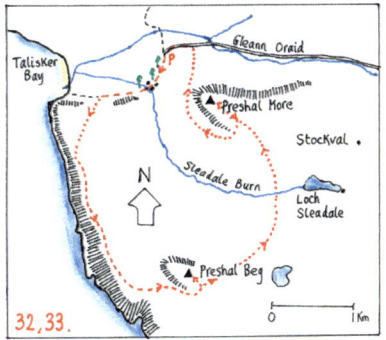

LONELY TALISKER BAY sees a constant trickle of visitors over the summer months and many will be surprised and amazed at the thrusting columns of rock forming Preshal More, totally dominating the immediate landscape. Its wee twin of Preshal Beg, oddly higher than Preshal More, is more shy and retiring, but on close inspection, just as rocky and imposing.

The name 'Preshal' is likely a cor-ruption of the Gaelic 'priseil' meaning 'precious'. Both hills have steep, rocky facades on three sides, mainly composed of columnar basalt, similar to that in Staffin (north Skye) and the island of Staffa. Each hill could easily be ascended separately, but it makes sense to include them both in a single outing, described here.

There is limited parking at the end of the public road in Gleann Oraid, opposite a track going right. Walk down the track, signposted 'to the beach',

Preshal More from Talisker

The fluted columns of Preshal Beg

past Talisker House. You will soon spot Preshal More off to the left, towering over the bay. Before reaching the end of the track, at the beach, turn off left to climb steep, grassy slopes, following the rough line of a stream. Do not attempt to climb the slope beyond this point, as there are steep crags.

Reach an area of flatter ground and veer right to the vicinity of the cliff edge, where sheep-cropped grass gives easier going. Enjoy fine vantage points back to Talisker Point with its sea-stack and also south to the immense cliffs of Biod Ruadh, your next objective.

Preshal Beg does not appear until you reach the high point on Biod Ruadh, where the fluted columns of basalt, forming its west and south face, are very prom-inent. The hill has a curious 'lost world' appearance, and in a certain light, can look quite intimidating and forbidding.

Descend Biod Ruadh, crossing a patch of boggy ground, before climbing up to gain close inspection of the hill's weird rock architecture. The only walk-ers' route to the summit is by a devious line on the south-east flank, where there is a break in the cliffs at a col, just to the left of an obvious rocky wart. For the more adventurous, there are a num-ber of exploratory scrambles, but, be warned; there is much loose rock, as the notable rockfall on this side indicates.

The summit area, marked by a cairn, is flat and somewhat of an anticlimax, but the views compensate. Descend by the ascent route to the col, before going left,

Preshal More from Preshal Beg

down a grassy ramp, avoiding the crags.

From here to Preshal More, it is a matter of contouring around the wide corrie of Sleadale, on sheep and deer tracks. You may also wish to visit the higher summit of Stockval, which is really the parent hill of Preshal More, but is relatively uninteresting. Stockval throws out a long, western spur, of which Preshal More is its abrupt and precipitous termination.

Cross the Sleadale Burn and head directly to Preshal More. The final rise is noticeably steep, at a break in the much steeper crags, and the summit is a few hundred metres further on. A smaller cairn, beyond the actual summit cairn, is the best viewpoint, perched on a rocky platform. You can sit, with your feet literally dangling over a sheer drop, and admire the bird's-eye view of wild Talisker Bay – an Eagle's Eyrie indeed.

Return by retracing steps down the steep section, then turning right to gradually descend a grassy depression. Follow the base of the cliffs round to the north side, at Buaile an Fharaidh, before dropping down to the road, just east of some crags. Turn left and reach the starting point in a few hundred metres.

Talisker Bay from Preshal More

34. BEN TIANAVAIG SMALL HILL AT THE HARBOUR (413M/1,355FT)

MAP	OS SHEET 23 (GR 512410)
DISTANCE	6KM
ASCENT	413M
TIME	3–4 HRS
ACCESS	CAMASTIANAVAIG
DIFFICULTY	EASY ASCENT ON AN INTERMITTENT PATH AND A GOOD RETURN COASTAL PATH.
SUMMARY	A beautiful, shapely coastal hill with excellent views across to Raasay, Portree and the east coast.

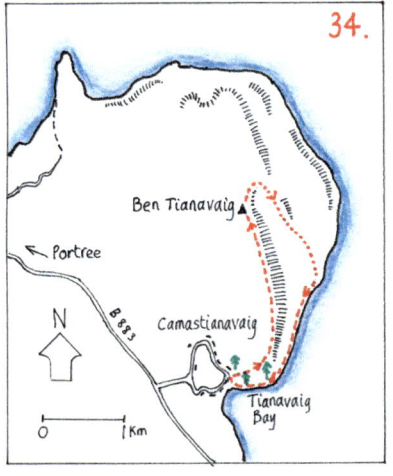

Ben Tianavaig from the north

ALTHOUGH NOT PART of the Trotternish Ridge, Ben Tianavaig's appearance and geology share much with the distinctive, stepped landscape found in the north-eastern part of Skye. The entire hill forms a remarkable cliff-girt peninsula, between Portree Bay in the north and Tianavaig Bay in the south.

The described route ascends the fine south ridge of the hill and returns by a coastal path, but some may prefer to just return by the ascent route.

Begin at Tianavaig Bay, at the little hamlet of Camastianavaig, and park at a small parking area near a picnic table. Walk about a hundred metres along the road, going uphill, and take the first track to the right at a bungalow. A sign indicating 'hill path' directs you up some steps and through a gate to a bracken-infested path, which leads up through some trees, to more open ground.

The path meanders its way up to meet the south ridge of the hill, at a height of around 100m – a flattish area, with crags overlooking a steep drop to the sea. From here, simply follow the crest of the obvious ridge, with a continuous line of steep slopes and cliffs on your right. This is a fine, exhilarating romp, for 2km, all the way to the summit, on a mostly obvious path and sheep-cropped grass.

The airy summit is crowned by a trig point and is a marvellous spot to while away a good half hour admiring the striking view across to the island of Raasay, with its distinctive summit of Dùn Caan (see Route 49). Portree Harbour and the eastern cliffs are also very prominent.

I always associate this hill with my wife, Heather, who lived at Camastianavaig for a short spell, while teaching in Portree. This is the only hill that she had climbed before me – and she is not a hillwalker by any stretch of the imagination!

To return by the coastal route, continue northwards, descending slightly, until, at a height of about 350m, drop down to the right at a break in the crags. Head in a roughly south-eastern direction to a flattish area, before descending more steeply, through landslipped terrain, to eventually reach a wide, grassy promontory on the coast.

From here, a fairly distinct coastal path heads south, staying about 15m above the sea, contouring along quite steep terrain, latterly below some cliffs, where care is needed. As you round the point to Tianavaig Bay, the path is often overgrown with bracken and also very uneven and boggy. In the latter stages it is better to follow the shoreline on pebbles and rocks until you reach the burn. Walk up to the road from here and cross the bridge to reach your starting point in only 50m.

The summit of Ben Tianavaig

MACLEOD'S TABLES

35. HEALABHAL MHÒR (471M/1,544FT)
36. HEALABHAL BHEAG (489M/1,604FT)

MAP	OS SHEET 23 (GR 220445, 225422)
DISTANCE	11KM
ASCENT	700M
TIME	5–7 HRS
ACCESS	NORTH OF ORBOST (GR 256445)
DIFFICULTY	PATHLESS, TUSSOCKY TERRAIN; TRICKY ROUTE-FINDING IN MISTY CONDITIONS
SUMMARY	A classic round of Skye's iconic twin peaks, best attempted in clear weather.

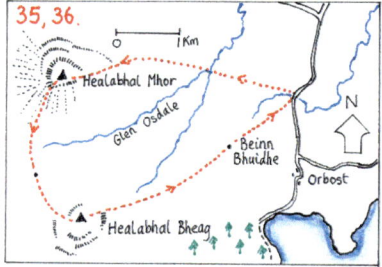

THE DISTINCTIVE FLAT-TOPPED hills known as MacLeod's Tables dominate the landscape of Duirinish in north Skye and are visible from many other parts of Skye.

The popular name, 'MacLeod's Tables', derives from a MacLeod chief, who was invited to dine in the palace of King James V in Edinburgh. On failure to express due admiration of his opulent surroundings, an earl pointedly asked: 'Have you ever seen in Skye halls so spacious as these, a roof so lofty, a table so ample and richly laden and candelabra so ornate as those around us tonight?'

The MacLeod chief replied that on Skye there was a far superior banqueting hall and invited the earl to come and see for himself. On arrival, he was taken at nightfall to the broad, flat top of Healabhal Mhòr, where a banquet was laid out. The chief said proudly: 'This is my table, larger and finer than yours, and these are my candlesticks', pointing to the hundreds of his clansmen with flaming torches, surrounding them. 'And this is my splendid ceiling', added the chief, holding his arm high to a star-studded sky.

In the face of such indisputable evidence, the earl was duly humbled and the MacLeod chief won the hearts and

Macleod's Tables from the east

minds of both Highland and Lowland aristocracy – hence the name. True story? Of course!

The individual hill names are a Norse/Gaelic mixture, with 'Healabhal' resulting from the Norse 'hellyr', a flagstone, or possibly 'hyalli', a terraced ridge and 'fjall', as in fell or hill. 'Mhòr' and 'bheag' are Gaelic, meaning big and little, respectively. Although Healabhal Mhòr has less height, it has greater girth and bulk than Healabhal Bheag. Other sources claim that their names derive from 'helgi fjall', meaning 'holy fell', due to their similarity to great natural altars.

On a more definite note, both hills are geologically the result of differential, basalt lava flows, producing the horizontal stratification and terraced landscape, also responsible for flat-topped Dùn Caan on Raasay (see Route 49).

The Tables are best tackled by doing a round of Glen Osdale, the vast corrie on the east side of the hills. This is best effected from a point on the road 1km north of Orbost. Another popular starting point is at the bridge over the Osdale river, south of Dunvegan, but is not so central for climbing both hills together.

From the road, head west across the moor to reach the Osdale river in just over 1km. Cross the river and turn slightly north, to gain the broad, east ridge of Healabhal Mhòr, following it upwards over short terraces. Before the summit plateau, a band of steeper

Healabhal Mhòr from Healabhal Bheag

Loch Bracadale and the Cuillin from Healabhal Bheag

crags can be negotiated by any one of a number of gullies and grassy rakes and/or optional scrambling.

The vast, flat summit plateau is a great contrast to the steep ascent slopes and the cairn lies away off on the opposite side of the mossy plain. Due to the flat expansiveness, the summit views are not brilliant, but improve significantly on Healabhal Bheag.

Descend in a south-westerly direction, on scree and heather, with only small rock steps, to reach the broad, grassy col of An Sgurran, in 1km. Climb a small hillock at the head of Glen Osdale and descend to a second col, before the final rise to Healabhal Bheag, on steep grass.

The summit area is not as extensive as Healabhal Mhòr, but the view south-east from the trig point is absolutely stunning, across glittering Loch Bracadale, with its flotilla of small islands and the dramatic backdrop of the Cuillin ridge beyond.

Descend by the north-east ridge, tending left to avoid a rock buttress, which looks very impressive from lower down. Go over several small knolls on tussocky grass, ending on Beinn Bhuidhe, from where it is only just over 1km to the starting point.

37. WATERSTEIN HEAD (296M/971FT)

MAP	OS SHEET 23 (GR 145471)
DISTANCE	6KM
ASCENT	250M
TIME	2–4HRS
ACCESS	RAMASAIG ROAD HIGH POINT (GR 162452)
DIFFICULTY	EASY BUT PATHLESS, GRASSY WALKING
SUMMARY	A coastal walk to one of the most dramatic and impressive high points on Skye's coastline.

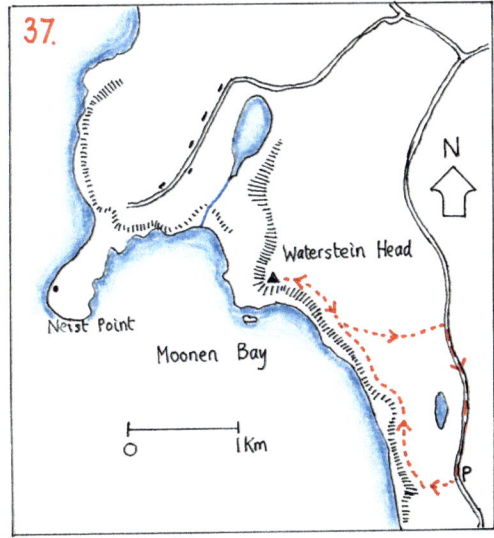

WATERSTEIN HEAD MAY not be the highest coastal hill on Skye, but its stupendous position overlooking the Neist Point peninsula (the most westerly point on Skye) gives it an air of aloofness and impregnability which is hard to resist.

An obvious route to the summit would be from the minor road to Neist at Loch Mor, where a natural line following the edge of the steep west-facing escarpment leads to the top in less than 2km. However, this route fails to reveal the true drama of the peak and a more satisfying and scenic route begins at the high point on the minor road to the tiny hamlet of Ramasaig. This no-through road has been neglected in recent years but is drivable with care.

Park at a suitable place on or near the high point and cut across west for about 300m to reach the coast. The view

A distant Waterstein Head from the south

from here, across Moonen Bay to the sheer cliffs of Waterstein Head backed by the Neist peninsula is breathtaking. Descend easy grass slopes and walk round an inlet, crossing a burn, before pleasant coastal walking follows the line of cliffs, gradually gaining height. As you near the summit, the direction changes to due west, following a fence for the last few hundred metres.

The trig point is unfortunately on the other side of the fence and it is up to the reader whether it is worth crossing! As a word of warning, there is a sheer drop beyond to the crashing waves of

Moonen Bay, but the view over to Neist Point can be appreciated without taking any risks.

If you do not need to return to your car, an ideal route is to continue north down the aforementioned escarpment line and reach the Neist road just north of Loch Mor. The best return route, however, is to retrace your steps south-eastward for about half a kilometre, before contouring round the southern flank of Beinn na Coinnich to reach the Ramasaig road just north of Loch Eishort. A kilometre road walk leads back to your car.

38. BIOD AN ATHAIR FATHER'S POINT (313M/1,027FT)

MAP	OS SHEET 23 (GR 158549)
DISTANCE	7KM
ASCENT	280M
TIME	3–4 HRS
ACCESS	GALTRIGILL ROAD END
DIFFICULTY	PATHLESS, TUSSOCKY MOORLAND; CARE NEEDED AT CLIFF EDGES
SUMMARY	An easy walk to the dizzying top of what is generally considered to be the highest sea cliff on Skye.

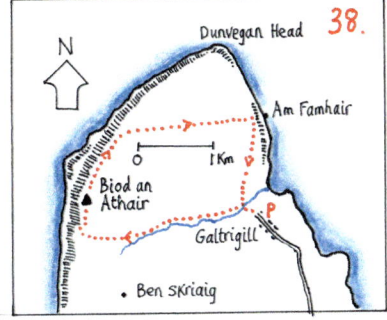

SOME SOURCES HAVE translated 'Biod an Athair' as 'sky cliff', despite 'adhar' being Gaelic for 'sky' and not 'athair', which means 'father', and 'biod' being a 'point' – not a cliff!

Whatever its meaning, this dramatic vantage point on the north-west coast of the Duirinish peninsula is a marvellous objective for those who love exposed cliff top walking and sensational situations. Although Sithean Bhealaich Chumhaing (see Route 39), north of Portree in east Skye, is higher above the sea, the cliffs are only vertical for a fraction of the height.

I first ascended this hill many years ago, during a long walk round Skye's coastline, approaching it from the south by the long line of cliffs, forming the entire western edge of the Dunvegan Head peninsula. This is undoubtedly the finest approach, but has logistical transport problems. The most convenient starting point is the end of the public road, on the east side of the peninsula at Galtrigill, where there is a parking area.

Strike off west, across heather moorland, following the line of the Galtrigill Burn. Ascend 150m in a little under 2km, to reach a broad col, north-west of Ben Skriaig. Contour round west from here, to reach the cliff edge in a few hundred metres. From this point, it is just under 1km to the top, and as you meander upwards, the sense of height and space become more pronounced.

The sheer cliffs of Biod an Athair

A few hundred metres short of the top, there is a sharp inward bend in the cliff edge, providing a stupendous view, looking up to the summit trig point, just a speck on the horizon.

After visiting the top, continue to follow the cliff edge for just over 1km, until it becomes less well pronounced. Some may wish to aim for Dunvegan Head, but as this has few distinguishing features, the recommended line is to head east, across the peninsula, on heathery moor, to the opposite coast, and the natural arch of Am Famhair (the giant).

The arch is unusual, by the fact that it is totally detached from the cliff face and stands like some giant sculpture on a raised beach. It is not entirely easy to locate but is more easily observed from the south.

From the arch cliffs, it is advisable to gradually ascend away from the coast, in a rising traverse, to avoid several gorges, formed by streams, including the Galtrigill Burn. Eventually, reach a path, which leads back to the parking area.

39. SITHEAN BHEALAICH CHUMHAING FAIRY HILL OF THE DEFILE, OR STRAIT (392M/1,287FT)

MAP	OS SHEET 23 (GR 509466)
DISTANCE	6KM
ASCENT	260M
TIME	2–3 HRS
ACCESS	TORVAIG
DIFFICULTY	INITIALLY, GOOD PATHS, FOLLOWED BY CLOSE CROPPED GRASS SLOPES
SUMMARY	This overlooked gem of a coastal hill is a fine objective for a summer evening, offering superb views.

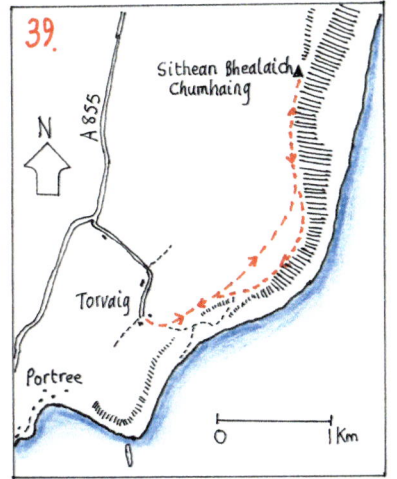

THIS GREAT WEE hill, standing north of Portree Bay, and easier to climb than pronounce, is the twin – and certainly no lesser cousin – of Ben Tianavaig to the south. It is less frequently climbed, certainly by visitors to Skye, but offers cliff scenery and vantage points to rival other, similar hills on Skye's coastline. I first ascended the hill from the north many years ago, during a complete Skye coastal walk (see Skye 360, Luath Press), but the inclement weather did little to extol the virtues of the hill. A recent evening's ascent in glorious sunny weather was a revelation, when the view of Ben Tianavaig was simply sublime.

Begin at the tiny settlement of Torvaig, lying 1km north-east of Portree and reached by taking the signposted minor road to the right, on the Staffin road,

The view south from Sithean Bhealaich Chumhaing

The summit of Sithean Bhealaich Chumhaing

north of Portree. Note that this road is north of Torvaig camping and caravan site. There is limited parking in Torvaig, just before the road goes downhill.

Walk down the road, passing a corrugated iron shed on the left, before turning left into what appears to be a cottage driveway. Go through a gate, with a 'path' sign, and fork right immediately, to follow a track. After going through a second gate, take a left turn, to follow an unmade track. Staying on the main track leads to the same point but involves more descent and re-ascent. The unmade path follows a field boundary, where cows often graze. At the end of the field, the two routes merge, before going steeply uphill and veering right, then left, in a wide arc, to reach an area of gentle slopes at Bealach Cumhang.

Moving off to the right brings you to the edge of the long line of cliffs, stretch-ing all the way from Portree Bay to Staffin in the north. The hill is the highest point of this extensive rocky bastion. The final kilometre to the summit offers myriad superb vantage points, looking down and along vertiginous cliff faces. On my recent visit, a pair of sea eagles were swooping and soaring, enjoying the thermals of a perfect summer evening.

The summit trig pillar is one of those dizzying, 'on the edge' viewpoints, where you are seemingly held in thrall to deliriously sublime vistas, and leaving is sacrilege. The finest views are south, to the bizarre, landslipped terrain of Ben Tianavaig, while Raasay dominates the seaward view. To the north is the unmistakable rocky finger of the Storr, on the Trotternish Ridge.

The return route can be varied slight-ly, by keeping to the cliff top as far as the steep ground, above the field.

40. BEN DEARG RED HILL (552M/1,811FT)

MAP	OS SHEET 23 (GR 478504)
DISTANCE	5KM
ASCENT	410M
TIME	3–4 HRS
ACCESS	CAR PARK NEAR 'BRIDE'S VEIL FALLS' (A855) (GR 495510)
DIFFICULTY	PATHLESS, ROUGH WALKING WITH SOME STEEP SECTIONS OF LOOSE EARTH AND SCREE
SUMMARY	An interesting ascent of a sadly neglected hill brimming with character at the southern termination of the Trotternish Ridge.

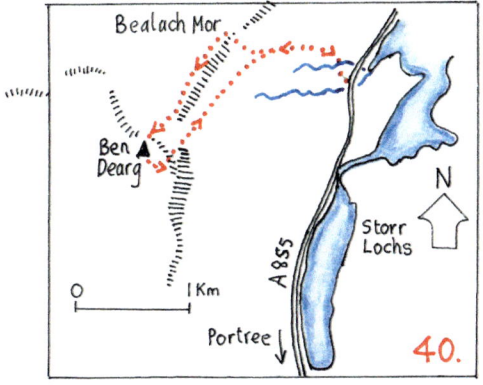

This route and the following eight are all hill ascents on or near the celebrated Trotternish Ridge, a 40km-long serpentine crest of east facing cliffs, pinnacles and buttresses and gentle, grassy west-facing slopes. The full two-day traverse of this ridge is a bucket-list expedition for many walkers and most of it forms part of the 'Skye Trail' long-distance route.

Ben Dearg is the southerly high point of the Trotternish Ridge, but as the crowds head for the popular Storr, several kilometres further north, Ben Dearg sees very few walkers, despite possessing some marvellous land slip features.

The small car park lies west of the Storr lochs but can often become busy, so you may need to try another lay-by some 700m north on the right. The route heads cross-country to Bealach Mor by first going through a gate and then north to a stream. Cross the stream and follow it west on grassy ramps. On approaching the bealach, stick to higher ground as much as possible, to avoid boggy sections.

Once at the bealach, turn left and

Ben Dearg from the north

follow the escarpment edge by a line of old fence posts. As you gain height the terrain steepens considerably and the relative safety of grass gives way to an unnerving mixture of loose earth, gravel and dodgy outcrops of rotten rock.

Thankfully, the gradient soon eases and grassy slopes lead to the cairned summit.

Descend south to a grassy col and turn left to descend steep grass slopes leading to a hidden defile guarded by a massive, castellated tower similar to those around the Quiraing. This is a marvellous, magical spot with grand views north to the Storr cliffs.

Follow a grassy ramp left of the tower, which runs alongside a long-eroded gully. Where the ground levels off, cross the gully and head directly for the line of approach, following it back to the car park.

Climbing Ben Dearg

41. SGÙRR A' MHADAIDH RUAIDH PEAK OF THE RED FOX (593M/1,946FT)

MAP	OS SHEET 23 (GR 474585)
DISTANCE	17KM
ASCENT	700M
TIME	6–8 HRS
ACCESS	LEALT (GR 508608) OR LEALT FALLS CAR PARK (A855) (GR 517605)
DIFFICULTY	EXCELLENT APPROACH TRACK AND PATHLESS, GRASSY HILLWALKING
SUMMARY	The bastion of cliffs forming the north-eastern aspect of Sgùrr a' Mhadaidh Ruaidh are almost as impressive as the Storr and Quiraing but receive few visitors. The route described here is a fine traverse of the hill, including the peaks of Creag a' Lain and Baca Ruadh.

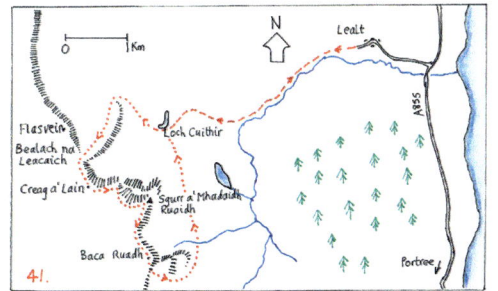

IT IS POSSIBLE to drive along the rough track from Lealt to Loch Cuithir (saving around 8km in total) but is not recommended unless in a suitable four-wheel drive vehicle. Limited parking is available at Lealt, but if this is not possible then use the Lealt Falls car park just south of the minor road to Lealt.

The track to Loch Cuithir was built to extract diatomite, a chalky marine sediment used in many industries, from in and around Loch Cuithir. Mining ceased in the 1960s, leaving a much smaller loch, a dismantled railway and the track you will be walking along.

As you approach the Trotternish Ridge along the winding, stony track, the imposing cliffs of Sgùrr a' Mhadaidh Ruaidh dominate the skyline. Distant views may give the impression of good scrambling and rock climbing potential, but the cliffs and buttresses are vegetated and plagued with loose earth and rotten rock to be avoided at all costs.

On reaching Loch Cuithir, stay on the

Sgùrr a' Mhadaidh Ruaidh from Loch Cuithir

track, as it winds round the southern side of the loch and head for the right-hand end of a low escarpment, which branches off from the main Trotternish Ridge. Keep to the left of a stream course and ascend easy grass slopes to the top of the escarpment. Head south-west along the crest, aiming directly for the Bealach na Leacaich on the Trotternish Ridge. The grass slope steepens considerably below the bealach, but numerous lines weave upwards, avoiding the rock outcrops, to reach the bealach and ridge.

Turn left and ascend easy slopes to the summit of Creag a' Lain, where there are magnificent views of the Sgùrr a' Mhadaidh Ruaidh cliffs. Descend eastwards to a col, then along the obvious grassy spur leading out to the small summit cairn of Sgùrr a' Mhadaidh Ruaidh. This is a truly magnificent, airy vantage point, perched right on the edge of a precipice, offering unrivalled views of the Trotternish Ridge in both directions.

The next summit of Baca Ruadh lies directly south and is accessed by a delightful amble round the curving rim of Coir' an t-Seasgaich. Beyond the summit, descend eastwards, leaving the ridge down steep grass slopes to reach a grassy shoulder at the top of Baca Ruadh's eastern buttress. Turn right here and descend easier grass slopes, gradually wending left round the foot of the buttress to the wide base of Coir' an t-Seasgaich. Cross the corrie to the lower slopes of Sgùrr a' Mhadaidh Ruaidh and descend directly to Loch Cuithir and the end of the approach track.

The summit of Sgùrr a' Mhadaidh Ruaidh

42. BIODA BUIDHE YELLOW TOP (466M/1,530FT)
43. CLEAT NORSE: 'KLETTR', MEANING ROCK (336M/1,102FT)

MAP	OS SHEET 23 (GR 439664, 447669)
DISTANCE	4KM
ASCENT	350M
TIME	2–3 HRS
ACCESS	BEALACH OLLASGAIRTE (QUIRAING CAR PARK) (GR 440679)
DIFFICULTY	STRAIGHTFORWARD GRASSY PATH TO THE SUMMIT OF BIODA BUIDHE; A STEEP GRASSY DESCENT IS REQUIRED TO REACH CLEAT
SUMMARY	A grand, short excursion to one of the finest viewpoints on the Trotternish Ridge, just south of the celebrated Quiraing, followed by an ascent of Cleat, a marvellous wee summit detached from the main ridge.

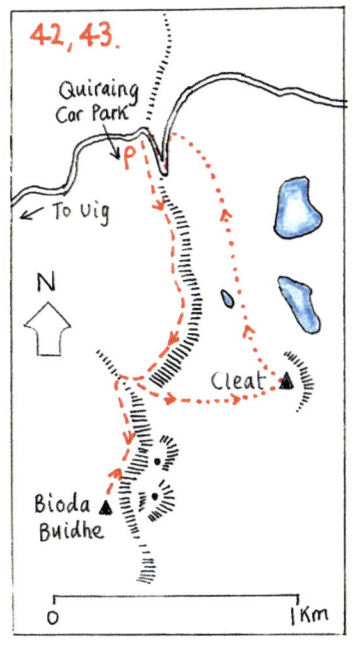

THESE TWO HILLS and the following five are all situated in the vicinity of the justly famous and popular Quiraing, an area of fantastic landslip terrain, resulting in a plethora of contorted pinnacles, secret defiles, castellated ridges and distinctive hills, seemingly created with the term 'Hugh' in mind. The name 'Quiraing' originates from the Norse 'Kvi rand' or 'Quoy rand', resulting in the Gaelic 'Cuith raing', literally translating as 'the pillared enclosure'.

Gone are the days when the Bealach Ollasgairte, on the narrow and hair-pinned Brogaig to Uig road, held a tiny car park and little more than a glorified sheep track led to the rock sanctuary of the Quiraing. Nowadays with Skye in the grip of mass tourism, a vast new

Bioda Buidhe and Cleat from the Quiraing

pay and display car park has since appeared– 'you pave paradise and put up a parking lot', and the Quiraing path is being upgraded as these words are being written.

The route to Bioda Buidhe leaves the potential crowds and heads in the opposite direction, southwards, following a fairly obvious path sticking to the escarpment edge, giving glorious views of the peaks and pinnacles of the Quiraing itself. Ignore a fork right about 500m from the start and stay on a path which clings to the cliff edge. The right fork still leads to the summit but adopts a more inland route passing through a metal gate and is not as scenic.

The higher you climb, the more the vistas open up and the view south becomes more dramatic with the craggy prominence of Cleat very obvious above its twin lochans. After 1km the escarpment swings round to the southwest via a series of high points and the dramatic pinnacled ramparts of Druim an Ruma and Dùn Dubh are well seen below the crumbling cliffs of Bioda Buidhe's eastern facade.

Descend and follow a fence where steepish grass slopes lead down to the area east of Cleat. Note that this is the descent route after climbing Bioda Buidhe. This break in the cliffs is one of only a few along the entire length of the Trotternish Ridge. The fence soon bends right uphill to a metal gate.

The view northwest from Bioda Buidhe to Cleat and the Quiraing

Follow uphill and go through the gate, continuing to follow the fence uphill on the opposite side. You will soon reach a fantastic vantage point with the cliffs of Bioda Buidhe plunging down to inky depths.

The actual summit of the hill is still a few hundred metres away round a bend in the escarpment but is very flat. No surprise that this Hugh gains its star for being a superb viewpoint.

To reach the detached summit of Cleat, return by your ascent route until above the grassy slope at the break in the cliffs. Pick your way carefully down the steep slopes for about 150m of descent before heading directly to the lower slopes of Cleat. Ascend grass slopes, tending left to avoid a craggy bluff about halfway up. Easier slopes soon lead to the flat summit where a narrow neck is traversed to a more distinct airy perch forming a grand seat and viewpoint.

To return to the car park, descend by the same route before turning north across heathery terrain, staying well above the twin lochans on the right. Reach the road in just over 1km and follow it round the hairpin bend to reach your starting point.

44. QUIRAING EAST PEAK (342M/1,122FT)
45. SRON VOURLINN NOSE OF THE POOL SPRINGS (380M/1,247FT)
46. MEALL NA SUIRAMACH POSSIBLY HILL OF THE MAIDEN OR SEA-NYMPH (543M/1,781FT)

MAP	OS SHEET 23 (GR 454692, 453708, 446695)
DISTANCE	8KM
ASCENT	230M
TIME	3–5 HRS
ACCESS	BEALACH OLLASGAIRTE (QUIRAING CAR PARK) (GR 440679)
DIFFICULTY	MAINLY EXCELLENT PATHS BUT WITH SOME INTIMIDATING SITUATIONS IF YOU ARE VISITING 'THE TABLE'
SUMMARY	A consistently interesting and varied expedition through the magnificent rock architecture of the Quiraing, and arguably the finest excursion on the Trotternish Ridge.

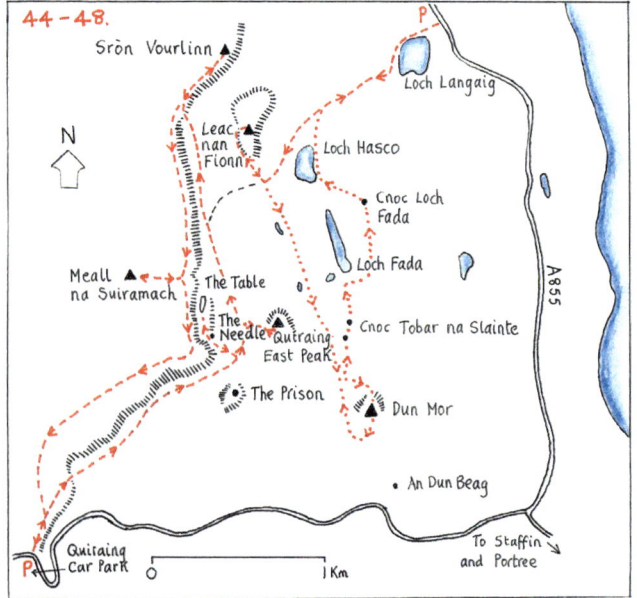

FROM THE CAR park follow the well-trodden and upgraded footpath which contours along the steep hillside, ignoring a left fork meandering its way upwards, eventually to Meall na Suiramach (this is your return route). Cross an awkward little stream gully – which may well be bridged by the time these words are in print – and continue along the obvious path hugging the hillside. After about a mile, reach the stony col and a cairn between the so-called 'Prison' on the right and the tottering spire of 'The Needle' on your left. The twin-towered castellated ramparts of the Prison may give the impression of a possible scrambling objective, but it should be emphasised that the whole Quiraing vicinity possesses much loose and dangerous rock and the Prison is no exception. Suffice to say that none of the Hughs described here involve any scrambling.

If you are interested in a thorough exploration of the Quiraing, leave the col at the cairn and head left up an eroded path which zigzags upward to the left of the Needle and in behind it to cross a gully. The path continues awkwardly between two rock towers and has a curious slot canyon feel, through a pinnacled defile, at the head of which is the third of the Quiraing's weird rock features (after the Prison and the Needle) – 'The Table'. This is an immense wall of rock with a vast, flat, grassy top, which can be accessed by heading along its base to the left. Enter a gap behind the Table, where a path leads to the flat top. This is a truly magical place for an extended stop and was reputedly used by the MacDonalds to conceal their cattle. Retrace your steps to the col

Quiraing East Peak from main path

between the Prison and the Needle.

The main path continues north over a large wooden stile, from where the first Hugh of the day makes a prominent appearance – the fine wee conical summit ahead on the right. Continue along the narrow path until almost opposite Quiraing East Peak, as it has been rather unimaginatively named, before descending to the right for about 30m to a boulder strewn col. Ascend the hill's easy lower slopes and steeper upper slopes on grass and heather to reach the tiny, airy summit, with barely room for two people. Revel in the fact that you are now standing on a rarely climbed Quiraing hill. Do not attempt to descend any other way than the route of ascent – dangerous crags prevail on the north and

Sron Vourlinn from the Quiraing path

The summit of Sron Vourlinn

eastern aspects of this summit.

Carefully retrace steps and climb back to the original path. Turn right and continue north, ignoring any right forking paths. Cross an old crumbling drystone wall and gradually begin climbing uphill below steep cliffs, eventually reaching a break in the crags, where a fence and stile marks Fir Bhreugach, the col on the Trotternish Ridge separating Sron Vourlinn (the next Hugh) from Meall Suiramach (the last Hugh). Cross the stile and turn right, following a path passing several dramatic pinnacles. Descend slightly, before the final easy plod to the remarkably exposed top of Sron Vourlinn. The name actually refers to the steep nose north of here, but has been adopted as the summit name. The summit is situated at a sharp bend in the ridge, with sheer drops to the south and east and as such, is a phenomenally exposed viewpoint, both seawards to the mainland peaks and southwards to the

Quiraing. The flat-topped 'lost world' type summit to the south-east is Leac nan Fionn, another Hugh described in the next route description.

Retrace steps to Fir Bhreugach and follow the ridgeline upwards on a good grassy path, from where there is an excellent view of Sron Vourlinn and its craggy defences. At a small cairn, turn right and walk away from the cliff edge on grass and moss for about 300m, to reach the trig point marking the summit of Meall na Suiramach. Rather like Bioda Buidhe, this hill's star rating is not for its prominence, but for its position and panorama.

Return to the cliff edge and head southwards, enjoying dramatic views looking down to the Table and surrounding rock spires of the Quiraing. Continue south-west above the cliffs following the grassy path as it contours across Maoladh Mòr, before finally descending to the path used on the approach. Turn right to return to the car park.

47. LEAC NAN FIONN FINGAL'S TOMBSTONE (380M/1,247FT)
48. DUN MOR BIG FORT (278M/912FT)

MAP	OS SHEET 23 (GR 453703, 459687)
DISTANCE	7KM
ASCENT	450M
TIME	3–5 HRS
ACCESS	QUARRY CAR PARK SOUTH OF FLODIGARRY ON A855 (GR 463710)
DIFFICULTY	EXCELLENT APPROACH AND RETURN PATH, BUT MUCH HEATHER BASHING AND 'YOMPING' IN BETWEEN!
SUMMARY	A walk connecting two excellent but fairly unfrequented Quiraing high points and also traversing another couple of interesting summits. Exploratory rambling at its best. Dun Mor may alternatively be climbed separately from the south, from the Uig minor road. See previous route for map.

THIS ALTERNATIVE APPROACH to the Quiraing is a breath of fresh air and a much quieter, more scenic offering than the tourist honeypot described in the previous two routes. Driving northwards on the main Portree road (A855), continue on past the Uig fork for about 2 miles to park at a small quarry on the left, just 100m past a footpath sign and large wooden 'Loch Langaig' sign. If this is full, there is another small parking area just south of the signs, with a path meeting the main path at Loch Langaig.

Leac nan Fionn from Loch Langaig

After only 100m of walking, reach the idyllic Loch Langaig, a popular spot for wild camping in the summer. It is from here that you gain your first glimpse of Leac nan

Leac nan Fionn from the south

Leac nan Fionn from Sron Vourlinn

Fionn, the seemingly impregnable fortress of a hill directly ahead. In his enchanting book *The Magic of Skye*, (published in 1949) the renowned photographer and hillwalker WA Poucher wrote:

> What appealed to me about Leac nan Fionn was that it appeared to be an isolated tableland whose ramparts seemed unscaleable, and whether I looked at it from Loch Langaig or from any of the nearby heights, I could discover no weakness in its defences.

Suffice to say that he did find a weakness and in fact the western aspect of the hill (facing the Trotternish Ridge) consists of a line of low crags with several easy grassy breaks in its armour.

Follow the excellent path round the north side of the loch, before gradually climbing for another half kilometre to reach a second scenic little lochan called Loch Hasco. Stay on the path as it climbs steadily, well above the loch,

with the huge, southern, rocky buttress of Leac nan Fionn now dominating the view to the right. At an obvious high point, just beyond a bend in the path, a faint grassy path breaks off to the right, heading up to the gap, left of the buttress. Follow this path, being careful not to mistake it for another path contouring round the base of the hill. Keep in mind that you are heading for the wide, grassy gap to the left of the buttress and make for the obvious drystone wall which crosses the gap higher up. As you approach the wall, keep to the right, directly underneath the sheer buttress, where the angle steepens considerably, on sometimes-loose shale and scree. Beyond a gap in the wall, the angle relents and, just beyond a minor col, the path goes directly up an easy grassy ramp to reach the plateau forming the summit area. Turn right and follow the edge for about 100m, before crossing over to the high point on the left and the true summit of this remarkable little hill.

View south from Leac nan Fionn

Like Sron Vourlinn to the north, the summit stands on the edge of a precipice and is a stunning viewpoint, especially southwards to other outlying satellite summits of the Quiraing, including Dun Mor, about 1.5km away to the south-south-west, your next objective.

Descend by the route of ascent and return to the main Quiraing access path. Almost immediately, leave the path to head south across heathery terrain, passing two small lochans and the sharp cone of Quiraing East Peak on the right. Descend slightly to more boggy ground marked on the map as Tobar na Slainte (an ancient well) from where Dun Mor is seen to advantage ahead on the left.

The described route climbs the steep northern face of the hill, avoiding an upper tier of crags on the left. If you prefer a gentler ascent, continue in a southerly direction and make an awkward crossing of a barbed wire fence to reach the grassier and less craggy south side of the hill. A small band of crags near the top can be circumvented on the left. Unfortunately, the same fence has to be recrossed to reach the true summit from this direction. For those ascending from the north, it is advisable to descend the south side, which will also entail an immediate fence crossing and another again on the west side for the return. For those ascending and

Staffin Bay from Dun Mor

descending from the south this will involve four crossings.

Despite the name Dun Mor (big fort), there are no obvious remains of such, but An Dun Beag (the little fort), visible to the south, possesses circular remains of a fort-like structure and is best visited from the Uig road. The best view from Dun Mor is east and south-east to Staffin Bay, Staffin Island and the village of Staffin itself, with its scores of sugar grain white cottages.

Looking north from the hill you will notice a nearby prominent summit with a south to north ridge line. This is Cnoc Tobar na Slainte and forms the first part of the return route. After first negotiating the fence, descend southward, avoiding a girdle of crags on the right. Bear right lower down and turn to head north, reclimbing the fence, before making for the grassy col, north of Dun Mor. Easy slopes then lead up to the interesting double-summited Cnoc Tobar na Slainte, whose highest point is the second summit at 281m. Continue north to a small hillock overlooking the ribbon-like Loch Fada and drop down to the right, going through a metal gate in the fence. Climb easy grass slopes forming the southern end of another fine wee hill, Cnoc Loch Fada, whose undulating summit area has a fine narrow ridge containing one of two high points. Yet another barbed wire fence has to be negotiated to reach the second high point at 274m.

Another small conical summit sits to the north of this hill, but the described route ignores this and drops easily down to Loch Hasco, following its eastern shore back to the main Quiraing path used on the initial approach. Head down the path to Loch Langaig and the road to complete a satisfying round of lesser known Quiraing hills.

RAASAY

49. DÙN CAAN (444M/1,457FT)

MAP	OS SHEET 24 (GR 579396)
DISTANCE	5KM
ASCENT	300M
TIME	1.5–2.5 HRS
ACCESS	GR 561406
DIFFICULTY	REASONABLY GOOD PATH ALL THE WAY TO THE SUMMIT
SUMMARY	A short walk to Raasay's highest point, the distinctive and iconic, flat-topped hill, prominent from many parts of Skye.

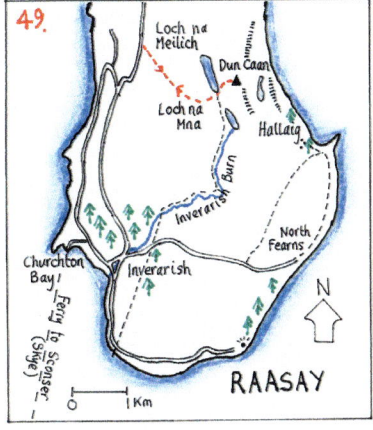

ON THE BASIS that many walkers will visit Raasay for just a day and may wish to include Calum's Road and a possible ascent of Beinn na h-Iolaire (see following route) in addition to Dùn Caan, the following route description is for the shortest, easiest ascent. For those with more time at their disposal and who may not have brought a car

to the island, there is a brief outline of optional, longer and circular routes at the end of the main description.

The name 'Dùn Caan' has suffered a historical letter-ordering error and is correctly 'Dùn Cana' in Gaelic. While the word 'dun' means 'hill fort', 'cana' translates as 'little whale' or 'porpoise', and with some imagination, the hill's profile could be likened to the dorsal fin of such a creature. On the other hand, some historical accounts link the name to Canne, cousin of a Danish king, or even to a Celtic prince, Cana Mac Gartnain – take your pick.

Great accumulations of lavas in north Skye and Raasay are typified by table-topped hills, such as Macleod's Tables in Duirinish (see Route 35, 36) and Dùn Caan in Raasay. It is interesting that much of Raasay escaped glaciation, resulting in extensive rare and ancient flora, especially on the steep,

Dùn Caan from Loch na Meilich

stepped terraces of the east coast.

Begin the walk up Dùn Caan at a point on the road north (GR 561406) where, at the time of writing, a small cairn and sign marked the start of the path. This is on the right side of the road as you drive north.

The path makes a gradual rising traverse of the hillside in a south-easterly direction, before turning east, over boggier terrain, to arrive at a tiny lochan. A fine view of the final slopes of the hill can be had from the much larger, adjacent Loch na Meilich. The Gaelic 'meilich' is 'chill with cold', so swimming is not advisable!

Follow the path round the southern end of Loch na Meilich and its continu-

ation up Dùn Caan's easy western flank. Near the top, there is some optional scrambling on a profusion of rocky outcrops. From the summit trig point, the views in all directions are truly magnificent, but especially south-west, across sparkling Loch na Mna (loch of the woman) to the sea, and Skye Cuillin beyond. Applecross, and the mainland, lie to the east.

James Boswell, on his famous tour of the Hebrides in 1773, found Raasay a delight, and on one particular morning, he rose before 6am, having a breakfast of dry bread and whisky, before setting off with Macleod, the laird, to climb Dùn Caan. He describes reaching the summit: 'where we sat down, ate cold

The summit of Dùn Can

The Red Cuillin from Dùn Can

mutton and bread and cheese and drank brandy and punch. Then we had a Highland song... then we danced a reel'. Whether the dancing of the reel was inspired by the sublime summit views, or charged by the effects of whisky, brandy and punch is not documented, but I suspect a combination of both!

Return by the outward route, unless you are unhampered with having to return to a car, in which case, pick up a southerly path, following the Inverarish Burn, leading down to Inverarish, Raasay's main settlement. This option, and others, are now briefly outlined.

Option 1: The western circuit

A circular walk can be made from Inverarish, by following the road north for 4.5km, past the Alan Evans Memorial Hostel, to the point where the ascent path starts (see above description). After descending Dùn Caan to the tiny lochan, turn left to follow the path on the west side of Loch na Mna and the Inverarish Burn, reaching the road at GR 565365. Turn right to Inverarish. The Inverarish Burn path is a popular ascent route and you may wish to complete this

circuit in reverse.

Option 2: The eastern circuit

Also from Inverarish, you can ascend Dùn Caan by the Inverarish Burn path, then descend to Loch na Mna, before leaving the path in a south-easterly direction, following the top of a line of cliffs. Beyond the cliffs, descend grassy slopes, to the famous Clearance settlement of Hallaig, a poignant reminder of brutal times and immortalised in Sorley MacLean's haunting elegy, 'Hallaig'. From here, a good coastal path and track lead to North Fearns and the road back to Inverarish. For those without a car, Inverarish is only 1km from the pier and ferry terminal in Churchton Bay.

GETTING TO RAASAY

Vehicle ferry from Sconser, Skye, to Churchton Bay, Raasay (Tel: 08000 66 5000). Several crossings daily (25 minutes).

50. BEINN NA H-IOLAIRE HILL OF THE EAGLE (254M/833FT)

MAP	OS SHEET 24 (GR 600503)
DISTANCE	7KM
ASCENT	260M
TIME	2.5–4 HRS
ACCESS	ARNISH
DIFFICULTY	GOOD PATHS FOR MOST OF THE WAY
SUMMARY	An easy walk to a summit, with a genuine 'end of the world' feel, plus an optional crossing to Eilean Fladday.

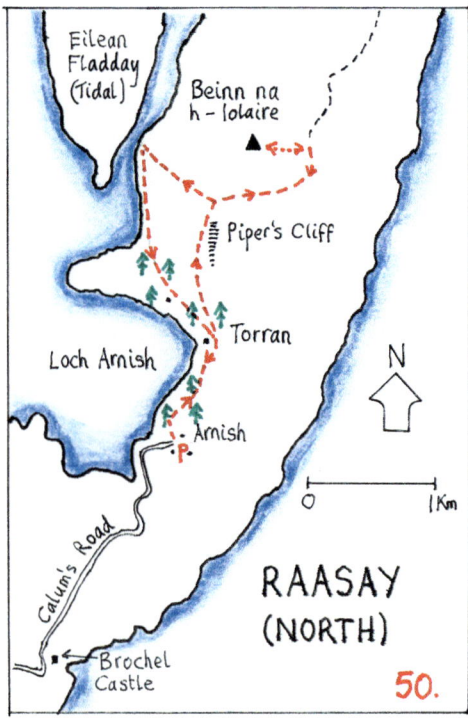

BEINN NA H-IOLAIRE MAY not possess the distinctive profile of Dùn Caan, but exudes a more elusive and alluring character, partly due to its differing geology and partly to its unique position on Raasay's northern gnarled finger, bestowing it with a more Outer Hebridean flavour. Whereas the southern part of Raasay is mainly Torridonian sandstone and granophyre, the north is Archaean gneiss, resulting in a landscape of bare, grey, sculpted crags and slabs and a more austere beauty.

North Raasay and South Raasay are connected by a narrow isthmus, barely 1km wide, containing the old township of Arnish, where the walk begins. However, you may want to start the walk 2.5km before Arnish, at Brochel, for good reason. Before

The summit of Beinn na h-Iolaire

the end of the 20th century, the public road ended at Brochel – until an Arnish resident, named Calum MacLeod, took his homemade wheelbarrow, a pick, an axe, a shovel and a three-shilling road-making manual and, over a backbreaking period of 10 to 15 years, constructed a road from Brochel to Arnish.

'Calum's Road', as it is now known, was built on the frustrations of one man with the County Council, whose dithering and delaying impelled Raasay's 'Local Hero' to embark on his monumental task. Television programmes have lingered over it; Scottish folk band, Capercaillie, have composed a Strathspey about it; art exhibitions have been inspired by it; and there has even been talk about a film being made of it. However you reach Arnish, admiration for Calum MacLeod and his remarkable, defiant gesture, will remain sure and undaunted.

At the end of Calum's Road, there is enough parking space for several vehicles. The route begins at a signposted track, forking left and meandering through natural woodland, for 1km to Torran. The building on the left here is the old schoolhouse, where Calum attended – who subsequently married the school mistress. At the schoolhouse, branch right on a path which climbs out of the woods onto open hillside. An impressive, steep crag on the right is known as Piper's Cliff, at the end of which you reach a fork in the path, with a small cairn. The left branch leads downhill to Eilean Fladday (or Fladda) and is your return route.

Branch right, to contour round the southern flank of Beinn na h-Iolaire, before rising to a high point of around 150m. Leave the path at this point, heading left (west), and after crossing hummocky terrain, with many crags and slabs, reach the summit trig pillar in only half a kilometre. The view north, to the rugged extremity of Raasay and across Caol Rona to the island of Rona is true unfettered wildness.

You can return exactly by the outward route or descend to Caol Fladda at the aforementioned path junction. Eilean Fladday is a tidal island and can only be reached across the causeway at low tide, but is worth visiting if conditions allow. The island used to accommodate four families, but now has only holiday homes.

To return to Arnish, follow an excellent coastal path for just over 1km – another of Calum MacLeod's creations – to rejoin the outward route at the old schoolhouse in Torran.

PART 2

THE NORTHERN ISLES AND OUTER HEBRIDES – 50 HUGHS

ORKNEY AND SHETLAND – 3 HUGHS
MINGULAY, BARRA AND ERISKAY – 4 HUGHS
SOUTH UIST, BENBECULA AND NORTH UIST –8 HUGHS
HARRIS/LEWIS AND SURROUNDING ISLES – 30 HUGHS
ST KILDA – 4 HUGHS

Castlebay from Heabhal (Barra)

The awesome western cliffs of Foula

Old Man of Hoy from the north

ORKNEY AND SHETLAND − 3 HUGHS

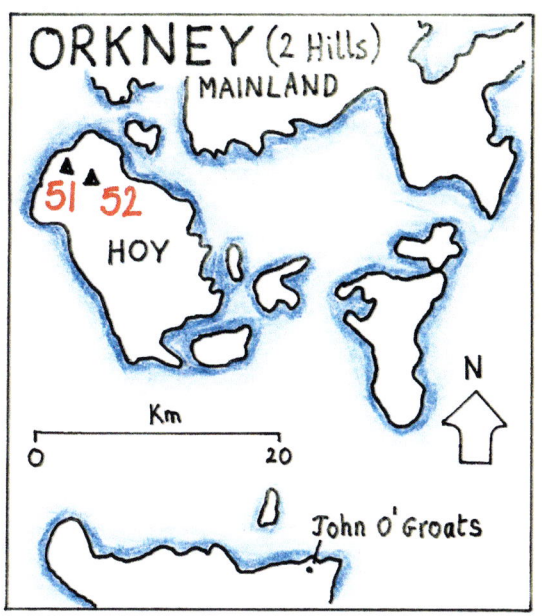

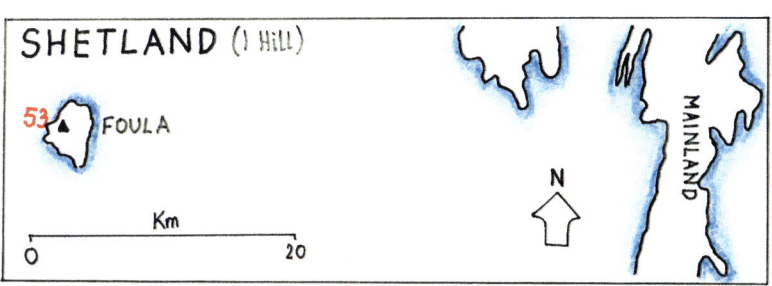

HOY, ORKNEY

51. CUILAGS (435M/ 1,427FT)
52. WARD HILL (481M/1,577FT)

MAP	OS SHEET 7 (GR 210033, 229022)
DISTANCE	20KM
ASCENT	950M
TIME	8–10 HRS
ACCESS	PASSENGER FERRY FROM STROMNESS TO MOANESS (GR 247040)
DIFFICULTY	A LONG AND CHALLENGING TRAMP ACROSS PARTLY PATHLESS TERRAIN, BUT ALSO GOOD PATHS
SUMMARY	This scenic circular route includes a visit to the infamous Old Man of Hoy and the coastal section is undoubtedly the highlight of the outing.

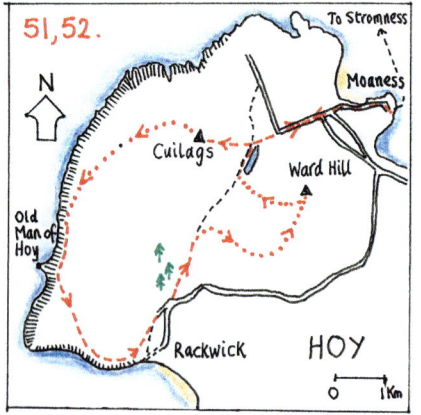

IT SHOULD BE noted at the outset that these two hills could be combined in a day's walk from Moaness, without the inclusion of the Old Man of Hoy. This would involve just over half the distance given above and reduce the time to around 5 hours. The shorter option is described within the text.

Hoy, the second largest of the Orkney islands, is by far the highest and wildest, and its name, originating from 'ha-oy', the Old Norse for 'high island', is quite fitting. Hoy is normally accessed from Houton, on Orkney Mainland, where a vehicle ferry goes to Lyness, in the south of the island. However, Moaness in the north is the best starting point for these two hills and a convenient passenger ferry from Stromness sails here.

Cuilags and Ward Hill are easily the most prominent hills in Orkney and are conveniently close together, providing a satisfying day out. There is another Ward Hill on Orkney Mainland, and the name originates from the Old Norse

Cuilags from Ward Hill (Hoy)

'*varda*', meaning a cairn, ward or look-out watch. Cuilags is simply the hill behind St John's Head, the huge sea cliff to the west.

At the time of writing, a passenger ferry to Moaness leaves at 7.30am from Stromness, arriving at 8am. Two return ferries leave Moaness at 4.30pm and 6.30pm, allowing up to 10.5 hours for the walk. It is advised to check ferry times online, or at Stromness ferry terminal, before going to Hoy.

From the tiny hamlet of Moaness, walk up the road for 2.5km, ignoring a right turn and two left turns. At the point where the road makes a sharp turn to the right, go straight ahead along a track to the weir at the north end of Sandy Loch. Ward Hill is directly to the left and Cuilags is straight ahead. Cross the weir and follow a vague path directly up Cuilags' heathery east ridge. After about 300m of ascent, several cairns appear in succession, the third one being the actual summit, after a narrow pencil cairn. On a clear day, this is a stupendous viewpoint out to Stromness, Scapa Flow and Orkney Mainland.

For those wishing to complete the shorter variation (omitting the Old Man), leave the summit in a southerly direction, to follow the broad south ridge down to the glen separating the two hills. Ward Hill is then best ascended by the route given later in the text.

Otherwise head north-west for half a kilometre to reach a broad, tussocky bealach, before heading south-west, gradually ascending in just over 1km to a trig point and shelter cairn. St John's Head, the top of the highest vertical sea cliff in Britain, is only a few hundred metres directly west of here and is best viewed from a promontory just north of this. However, the finest feature of the walk is the Old Man of Hoy itself, which still lies 3km south of here, across very tussocky and sometimes boggy terrain. As you approach the Old Man, a path begins to appear, near to the cliff edge, and the amazing, tottering, sandstone monolith can be viewed easily from numerous photogenic vantage points.

Leave the vicinity of the Old Man of Hoy by the popular access path, which winds round the hillside giving grand views of Rackwick Bay. Reach the road at a hostel and follow it until a short distance beyond, where another road branches off to the beach. A small footpath sign on the left indicates the path to be followed, between the two hills. This path, overgrown in places, crosses two bridges and leads to a copse of trees and bushes, after 1km. Once through the trees, leave the path and head directly up the west-facing lower slopes of Ward Hill, on tussocky heather and grass. This is now on the same route as the shorter option.

Reach a broad shoulder and continue to ascend, eventually reaching the top of the cairned subsidiary south summit of Ward Hill. The actual summit is still over 1km away along a wide stony ridge, passing several false summits. The true top is crowned by a trig point and is another magnificent viewpoint. If you are not rushing to catch the ferry, it is worth spending some time here.

Do not attempt to descend north from here, as there is a band of steep crags on the lower slopes. Instead, head directly west and then north-west, making a beeline for Sandy Loch and the path at its south end. Reach the weir and follow the track and road back to Moaness, to complete a satisfying and hopefully enjoyable day.

GETTING TO ORKNEY

Northlink Ferries offer a service from Scrabster to Stromness. Pentland Ferries also offer a service from Gills Bay in Caithness to St Margaret's Hope in South Ronaldsay. See websites for details. Flights are also available to Kirkwall with Loganair from Glasgow, Edinburgh, Dundee, Inverness and Aberdeen. See Loganair website for details.

For access to Hoy see details in text.

FOULA, SHETLAND

53. DA SNEUG OLD NORSE: 'KNJUKR' – STEEP CONICAL MOUNTAIN (418 M/1,372FT)

MAP	OS SHEET 4 (GR 948395)
DISTANCE	12KM (ROUND TRIP FROM HAM); 6KM (DIRECT FROM AIRPORT)
ASCENT	700M (ROUND TRIP FROM HAM); 420M (DIRECT FROM AIRPORT)
TIME	4–6 HRS (ROUND TRIP FROM HAM); 3–4 HRS (DIRECT FROM AIRPORT)
ACCESS	HAM PIER OR AIRPORT (SEE END FOR FOULA ACCESS)
DIFFICULTY	MAINLY EXCELLENT, GRASSY HILLWALKING, THOUGH STEEP IN PLACES ON THE LONGER CIRCUIT; EXTREME CARE NEEDED AT CLIFF EDGES; TREKKING POLES ARE A GOOD IDEA TO WARD OFF MARAUDING BONXIES
SUMMARY	The full circuit of Foula's main coastal high points on a clear day is the stuff of dreams and as unique an experience as you could wish for in the British Isles.

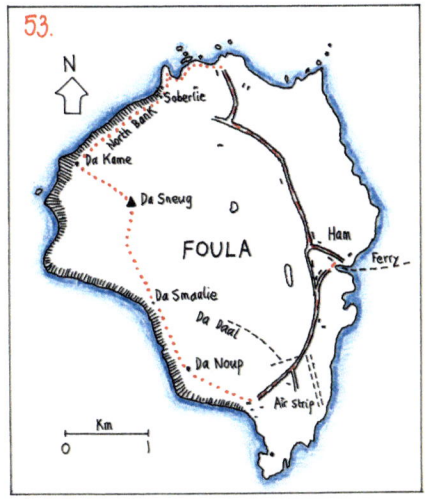

FOULA VIES WITH St Kilda and Fair Isle as one of the remotest islands in Britain, lying around 40km west of West Burra in Mainland Shetland. As such, it is highly susceptible to the vagaries of the unpredictable Atlantic airstreams and even reaching Foula can be something of a challenge.

Foula has many similarities to Hirta, St Kilda, both possessing immense cliffs and conical hills on one side of the island and gentler, low-lying land on the other. Unlike Hirta, however, Foula has retained a permanent population of around 35 inhabitants, involved in such diverse

Da Noup from the lower slopes of Da Sneug

occupations as teaching, nursing, ferry and fire crew, rangers and of course, crofting. The island is completely off grid and runs a hybrid electricity scheme, involving a few wind turbines, a hydro generator and solar panels.

The short, direct route to Da Sneug from the airport ascends the long, easy south-west ridge, over two subsidiary tops, before reaching the summit. This does not do justice to the hill however, and it is highly recommended that you consider the longer, circular route.

The following route description is dependent on having a full day on the island, which may not be possible if you are flying, or relying on the regular ferry from Walls on Mainland Shetland (see end for more details). It is highly recommended that you book with the tour company 'Shetland Sea Adventures', who offer almost 7 hours ashore, with the added bonus of a sea tour round the island and a three-course seafood meal on the island! If you only visit Foula once, which for most people will be the norm, then an approach to the highest point of Da Sneug, via the dramatic north side of the island, with its dizzying cliffs and awesome stacks and arches, is undoubtedly the classic route to the summit and shouldn't be overlooked.

On the approach to Foula by boat, from Shetland to the east, the island appears as a vast breaking wave, with the immense western cliffs essentially hidden from view. The whole of Foula's eastern side is a gentle, undulating, fertile plain, backed by the grassy slopes and ridges of its two main hills, Da Sneug and Da Noup. A minor road runs south to north, along this plain, with the berthing point at Ham Voe connecting to it via another minor road, halfway along the east coast.

If you are lucky (as I was), you may be offered a lift up to the north end of the island, saving over 2km of tarmac bashing. As you approach the road end, the distinctive west ridge of the first high point of Soberlie appears on the left. It may be tempting to ascend this easy-angled ridge, but this misses out on close viewing of some grand coastal features, reached by taking a right fork northwards towards a scattering of houses. Walk directly to the coast to view Gaada Stack, an outstanding double arched sea-stack, some 40m from the coast.

Follow the coastline to the left (west) to admire several other stacks and unusual rock formations, including

The summit of Da Sneug

The author at the foot of Soberlie
(Photo: Ruaraidh Dempster)

a second natural arch under a sharp promontory, below the steep, grassy ascent up to Soberlie. This ascent is much steeper than the aforementioned west ridge – almost grass scrambling in places– but following the cliff edge gives some beautifully exposed situations and a chance for puffin spotting. Consummate hill gangrel, the late Tom Weir, wrote:

Soberlie Hill is the most dramatic climb you can do on Foula, because the edge of Soberlie is a cliff, rising with every foot of ascent until you land on North Bank leading to the celebrated Kame, greatest precipice of Foula.

At the top of Soberlie, the North Bank is a grand kilometre of level cliff edge walking, with more opportunities for observing puffins. We were lucky enough to meet a lone Shetland pony, just before the next steep, grassy climb to Da Kame, for us, sadly, cloaked in mist. This 170m climb takes you to the top of one of the highest sea cliffs in Britain, second only to Conachair in St Kilda and 'more frightening than anything on St Kilda in my opinion' according to Tom Weir. I will have to take his word for that, as we were enveloped in mist.

The rock fissure of Da Maollie

south-east ridge, over two small subsidiary tops, followed by a long easy-angled spur, leading directly to the landing strip. This forms the reverse of the shorter, direct route from the airport.

To continue the longer walk, descend roughly south, down easy, but tussocky terrain, heading towards the obvious conical hill of Da Noup. This is great skua territory and these sometimes aggressive 'bonxies', as they are known, compete fiercely with arctic skuas for prime breeding areas. They will dive bomb anyone venturing too close to their nests, so it is a good idea to wave a trekking pole above your head to ward them off. Foula's Old Norse name was '*Fugla-ey*', meaning 'bird island' and in fact the island has the world's largest population of these aerial predators.

Between Da Sneug and Da Noup lies the flat glacial trough of Da Daal, at the western end of which is an extraordinary rock fissure known as Da Sneck ida Smaallie. This impressive rocky cleft is over 30m deep and was formed when a large block of sandstone detached from

Leave the coast here and head in a south-easterly direction down easy slopes of grass and sphagnum moss, before a slightly steeper and shorter ascent leads, in under 1km, to the cairn and trig point at the summit of Da Sneug. In clear weather, the whole west coast of Shetland and even Orkney is visible. I could only imagine such a scene. The remainder of the walk, including the second hill of Da Noup, could be curtailed here, by taking the obvious the cliff face, opening up a 2m wide dank and gloomy crevice. This is best viewed from its eastern extremity and is passed en route to Da Noup. It is not advised to attempt a descent into the cleft!

The option of heading east along Da Daal presents itself here, or continuing to follow the coast, by ascending the 248m high Da Noup, another fine wee hill (and a Marilyn). The summit of Da Noup gives a good retrospective view of Da Sneug and is the last high point of the day. Descend south-east on easy grass slopes to reach the road end. If there is time, you may wish to make the half kilometre diversion south to visit the lighthouse. A 2km road walk north leads back to Ham and the pier, to complete a unique and memorable excursion.

GETTING TO FOULA

Sea or air travel to Foula is totally dependent on agreeable weather, with low cloud, crosswinds and turbulent seas all contributory factors in making access problematic.

As mentioned in the text, the company, Shetland Sea Adventures, offer a full day on the island (summer only) and are highly recommended. They also allow a window of 3 to 4 days for sailings, so make sure your plans are fairly flexible. See their website for details. Note that prior booking is essential.

A regular ferry sails between Walls (Mainland Shetland) and Foula, with the timetable updated seasonally. For more information see the Shetland Islands Council website.

Airtask offer regular flights to Foula from Tingwall, weather depending. For more information and a timetable see the Airtask website or call the airport booking line on +44(0)1595 840246.

GETTING TO SHETLAND

Northlink Ferries run a service from Aberdeen to Lerwick some of which stop at Stromness. See website for details. Flights are also available to Sumburgh from Glasgow, Edinburgh and Aberdeen.

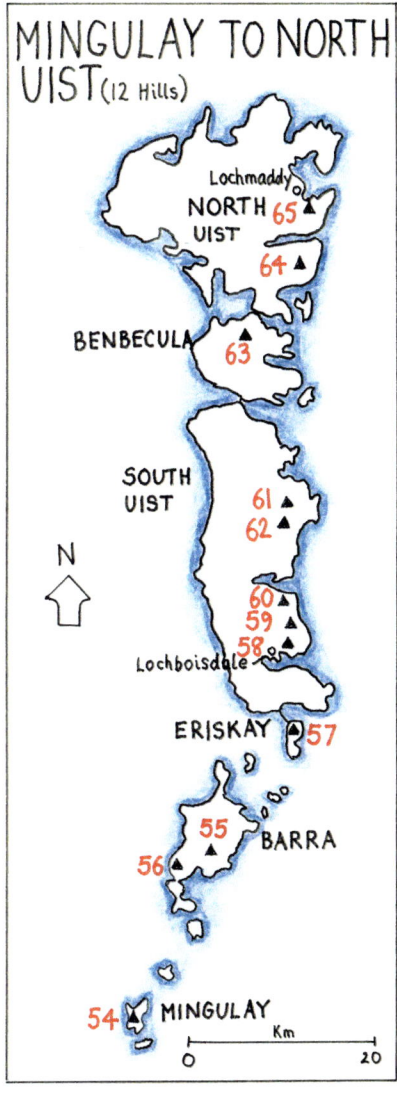

54. CARNAN THE CAIRN (273M/896FT)

MAP	OS SHEET 31 (GR 553828)
DISTANCE	6KM
ASCENT	380M
TIME	2–3 HRS
ACCESS	MINGULAY BAY (SEE BELOW FOR MINGULAY ACCESS)
DIFFICULTY	A PATHLESS, GRASSY AND TUSSOCKY WALK; A TREKKING POLE IS ADVISABLE FOR WARDING OFF GREAT SKUA ATTACKS (SEE TEXT)
SUMMARY	An exhilarating circuit of Mingulay's hills, offering dramatic views of the precipitous sea-stacks and cliffs of the west side.

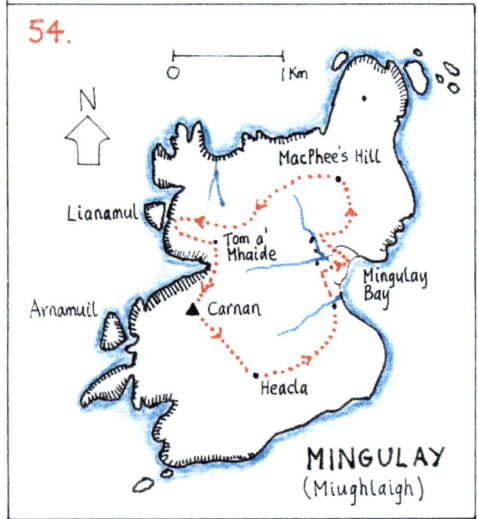

OWNED BY THE NTS, Mingulay is the largest of the five main islands south of Barra and Vatersay, and is also geologically and historically the most interesting. Uninhabited since 1912, the island has a St Kilda-like quality, with its vast cliffs and sea-stacks on the more exposed west side and a sandy, sheltered 'Village Bay' on the east side.

The described route takes in the three main summits of the island, the highest being Carnan, the middle summit, but for those with more limited time or ambition, it is still possible to climb Carnan and view the dramatic cliffs and stacks in only 1 to 2 hours.

Most landings on Mingulay are at Mingulay Bay (Village Bay) on the east side, and it seems almost sacrilegious to defile the laundered whiteness of the island's only beach with boot prints, as you wander up to the crumbling ruins of the long since deserted village. In his fas-

Mingulay Bay

cinating book, *The Road to Mingulay*, Derek Cooper remarks:

> I've been on many deserted Hebridean islands, but none so powerful a feeling of Humanity about it as Mingulay. The houses are so close one to another that you can almost catch the hum of conversation, see the peat smoke rising, hear the lowing of cattle and the cries of children playing…

Head up to the top of the village, passing the chapel house, before ascending the south-eastern flank of MacPhee's Hill on tussocky grass. The hill takes its name from a young rent collector who landed on the island to find all the residents dead. In his immaturity, he rushed back to the boat, still moored some distance away, and shouted that there was a plague on the island. Fearing that young MacPhee was now also infected, they rowed away without him. Some sources say that he survived a whole year on the island, but probably closer to the truth is 6 weeks, living on shell-fish and sheep. Every day he climbed 'MacPhee's Hill' to spot a passing boat. Thankfully, the story has a happy ending, with MacPhee being rescued and his family given free rent for the rest of their lives in compensation.

Descend west from MacPhee's Hill, then south-west, on a broad, grassy ridge, before traversing round the north flank of Tom a' Mhaidhe. By this stage, you will doubtlessly become acquainted with the massive sea birds known as great skua (bonxies), noted for their swooping, diving attacks on anyone they regard as being too close to their nests. A trekking pole held above the head is good for fending them off!

The cliffs north of Carnan

Pabbay and Barra from Mingulay

The fine sea-stack of Lianamul is so close to the cliffs, it was once connected to Mingulay by a rope bridge. From Lianamul, it is an easy plod to the summit of Tom a' Mhaidhe, sitting above the vast cleft of Bàgh na h-Aoineig, from the head of which there is a breathtaking view of Biulacraig, the highest cliff on Mingulay, rising sheer from the sea for over 200m.

It was here that I was amazed to meet up with a certain Julie Brooks, a wilderness artist, who had spent 6 months living in a cave on the remote west coast of Jura, painting and sculpting. There had been a television documentary of her living alone on Mingulay for 6 months and she was now here again with her family, living in the island's only bothy, owned by the NTS.

The highest summit of Carnan is a short, grassy climb to the south, with its trig point and glorious sea views in all directions. You may wish to descend south-west from here, to view another amazing sea-stack (Arnamul), and a natural arch which we were lucky enough to sail through, courtesy of our intrepid boatman! Otherwise, descend south-east to the final hill of Hecla, before easy grass slopes lead down past the NTS bothy and Mingulay Bay.

GETTING TO MINGULAY

Several boat tour operators work out of either Castlebay or Vatersay giving up to 3.5 hours ashore. One of the cheapest is Mingulay Boat Trips at only £50 per person (at the time of writing!). Try also Hebridean Sea Tours. Check online for availability.

BARRA

55. SHEABHAL (OR HEABHAL) POSSIBLY 'SEA HILL' (383M/1,256FT)

MAP	OS SHEET 31 (GR 678994)
DISTANCE	6KM
ASCENT	450M
TIME	2.5–4 HRS
ACCESS	CASTLEBAY (FOR BARRA ACCESS, SEE END OF FOLLOWING ROUTE)
DIFFICULTY	INDISTINCT PATHS, BUT GENERALLY STRAIGHTFORWARD
SUMMARY	Sheabhal, the highest point on Barra, is arguably one of the finest viewpoints from any hill in the Outer Hebrides. A circuit, including Thartabhal (Hartaval), is an ideal excursion.

MOST WALKERS WHO visit Barra will probably not have a car, so the route description begins at the pier in

Castlebay, Barra's main centre of population and the ferry port.

Walk up to the main road and turn right, reaching the highest point of the road after about 1.5km. There is a small car park here and is the normal starting point for the ascent of the hill. Cross a footbridge, then a stile over the fence and bear right on an indistinct path, which soon climbs directly upwards through heather and the odd rocky outcrop. After about 150m of ascent, reach a white, marble statue of the Madonna and Child, erected in 1954 and an iconic symbol of Barra's Catholic heritage.

This is a marvellous spot to absorb the magical view of the scattered township of Castlebay, Kiessimul Castle

Castlebay from Heabhal

and the tapestry of islands beyond, their white strands gleaming in turquoise seas. Another 100m of ascent brings you to the summit trig point and more excuse to just relax and drink in the surrounding splendour.

Head north from the summit, gradually descending to a grassy col, before traversing a secondary summit and cairn. Turn west and descend to a lower col, before following a path up the craggy eastern slopes of Thartabhal, another fine viewpoint. Descend to the south-east by a broad, initially level ridge, which soon drops down through heather and rocky outcrops. Gradually veer right to a level shoulder, before the final descent to the road, passing some standing stones. Turn right and reach the parking area in 1km.

56. BEINN TANGABHAL TONGUE HILL (333M/1,093FT)

MAP	OS SHEET 31 (GR 639991)
DISTANCE	7KM
ASCENT	330M
TIME	2.5–4 HRS
ACCESS	HALAMAN BAY (BÀGH HALAMAN)
DIFFICULTY	MAINLY ROUGH, PATHLESS WALKING
SUMMARY	A beautiful circuit, on a marvellous coastal hill.

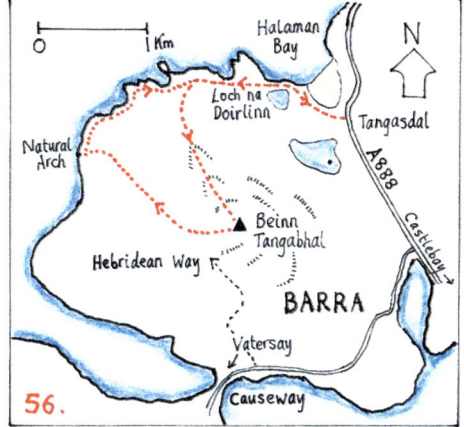

BEINN TANGABHAL STANDS in splendid isolation, in the south-west corner of Barra and north of the island of Vatersay (Bhatarsaigh). Consequently, its summit views easily rival that of Sheabhal.

The name Tangabhal translates as 'tongue hill', so the odd addition of 'Beinn' (hill) is a tautological oversight.

Begin the walk at Tangasdal, at Halaman Bay, which is about 3km north-west of Castlebay. The walkers' Hebridean Way route reaches the road at this point, and you can follow this way-marked route almost to the summit. Though not an actual path, the route is reasonably well shown by marker posts, which follow the coast for nearly 2km, before heading uphill.

Walk past the southern part of the bay and round the north of Loch na Doirlinn (loch of the isthmus). Climb slightly, through rocky terrain, aiming for Dun Ban, the remains of an Iron Age fortification, from where there is a grand view looking back across Halaman Bay to Beinn Mhartainn.

From here, the obvious craggy north-west ridge of Ben Tangabhal rises up directly to the summit and is the best as-cent route. The Hebridean Way follows

Heabhal and Castlebay from Beinn Tangabhal

the dip to the right of the ridge, which is also a perfectly feasible ascent route. The ridge is easy walking, through short heather and rock outcrops and leads naturally to the summit trig point. Enjoy glorious views of Castlebay, Sheabhal and also of the island of Bhatarsaigh to the south.

To make an interesting circuit, descend west from the summit to a level area, before turning north-west to descend an easy-angled heathery ridge. At the point where the ridge drops more steeply, at a height of about 150m, veer left (west) to Doirlinn Head, where there is a fine natural arch. Following the coast from here, you will pass other arches and intriguing coves, before again reaching Dun Ban. Follow the outward route to return to Halaman Bay.

GETTING TO BARRA

Vehicle ferry: Oban to Castlebay, every day in summer; Lochboisdale to Castlebay, 3 days a week. (Tel: 08000 66 5000). Eriskay to Barra: frequent daily service.

Air service: Glasgow to Barra and Benbecula to Barra, daily except Sunday (Tel: 0870 850 9850).

ERISKAY (Eirisgeigh)

57. BEINN SCIATHAN WING OR WINGED HILL (186M/610FT)

MAP	OS SHEET 31 (GR 797112)
DISTANCE	6KM
ASCENT	190M
TIME	2–3 HRS
ACCESS	BARRA FERRY SLIP ROAD (GR 786104)
DIFFICULTY	PATHLESS, GRASSY TERRAIN, WITH ROCK OUTCROPS
SUMMARY	A fine circuit of a delectable small island hill, including a grand beach walk to finish.

SOME WOULD MAINTAIN that Eriskay ceased to become an island on 12 July 2001, when the last ferry connecting the island to Uist ran, and the new causeway became a reality. In my own eyes and many others, I suspect, Eriskay is still an island, but just easier to access.

The ferry link to Barra is now only one of two ferry links wholly in the Western Isles, the other being the link from Uist to Harris. The small parking area on the right, just before the Barra ferry terminal, provides the starting point for this fine circular walk.

Walk up the road, away from the ferry, and turn right at the junction. In 250m, turn left up a track to reach a water treatment plant, situated just below Loch Cracabhaig – Eriskay's water supply. A vague path leads off to the left and is often boggy. Follow this path and cross a fence, with Loch Cracabhaig appearing on the right.

Ascend the hill by any desired route, weaving your way up a maze of grassy runnels and excellent pockets of rough gneiss crags and slabs to the summit trig point perched on a craggy knoll. This is a marvellous viewpoint down to the green sward, peppered with white cottages; and out over the causeway to the Uist hills.

Descend north-west on a broad, grassy spur for 1km, before heading directly in the direction of the small islet of Calbhaigh. Cross a fence and reach an old track and ruined shielings. Turn left to reach the road end in under 1km.

Follow the single-track road through the small hamlet of Haunn and past the causeway road, before making a right turn to reach 'Am Politician', a pub opened in 1988. It is named after a ship which sank off the aforementioned Calbaigh island in 1941, shedding its load of 24,000 cases of whisky,

Beinn Sciathan

View north from Beinn Sciathan

many of which were acquired by the Eriskay locals. The story was hilariously narrated in Sir Compton Mackenzie's *Whisky Galore* and dramatised in two subsequent films, one relatively recent.

After possible liquid refreshment in the pub, turn right and follow Hebridean Way signs past the old cemetery, taking a right, then left fork to a car park and a path leading down to the beach. Stride out along the sweeping stretch of sand, known as Coilleag a' Phrionnsa, (Prince Charlie's Bay) where Bonnie Prince Charlie landed from France in 1745, with the intention of gathering the clans for his rebellion.

In less than 1km, reach the end of the beach and follow the path upwards to the parking area at the start of the route.

58. BEINN RUIGH CHOINNICH HILL OF THE MOSSY ARM (280M/920FT)
59. TRIUIREBHEINN BOWL HILL? (357M/1,170FT)
60. STULABHAL HILL OF THE SHIELING HUT – NORSE (374M/1,228FT)

MAP	OS SHEET 31 AND 22 (GR 807197, 812212, 807241)
DISTANCE	14KM
ASCENT	720M
TIME	6–8 HRS
ACCESS	LASGAIR (GR 786202)
DIFFICULTY	VERY ROUGH, TUSSOCKY AND USUALLY BOGGY, PATHLESS TERRAIN
SUMMARY	A demanding, but satisfying, tramp over the three main coastal hills north of Lochboisdale (Loch Baghasdail). The option of leaving Stulabhal as a separate expedition is also considered.

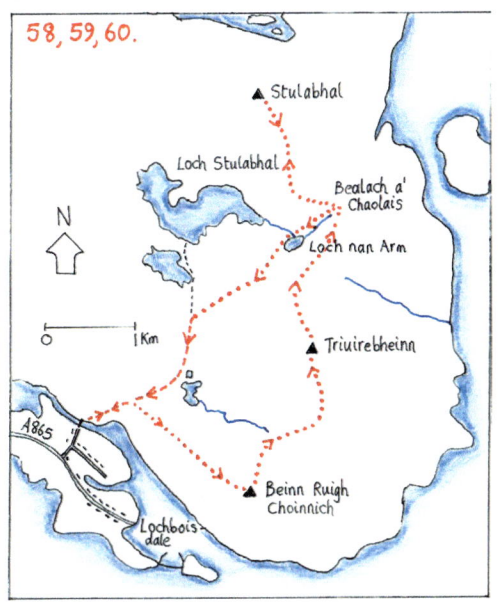

ALTHOUGH SIGNIFICANTLY LOWER than the complex Beinn Mhòr massif lying north of Loch Aineort, these three hills provide wild isolation, historical interest and views, which will more than repay the effort involved. There is also the option of returning to the start after the ascent of Triuirebheinn and a brief outline of a separate ascent of Stulabhal is given.

From the A865 Lochboisdale road, take the left turn for Lasgair at Braelee Guesthouse and park anywhere along this road. Follow the

Beinn Ruigh Choinnich

grassy track left, past two houses and continue down a grass lane, which becomes very boggy until the two-gate bridge over the outflow of Loch a' Bharp. Cross the bridge and follow an indistinct quadbike track for about half a kilometre, before heading south-east to the lower slopes of Beinn Ruigh Choinnich, now dominating the view ahead.

After 1km, the gradient steepens considerably; climb directly up in deep heather, staying left of an obvious large crag. The summit area is a confusion of separate tops, but there is a large cairn on the main summit with fine views. Lochboisdale sits directly below the hill, north of the protective sea loch.

Head north from the summit and descend easily to Bealach an Easain, directly below the complex southern face of Triuirebheinn. Weave up this face on grassy ramps and terraces, avoiding the craggy sections. Reach a flat shoulder, before ascending steep grass to the broad summit area, hosting a small cairn.

The final hill of Stulabhal lies around 3km to the north, across complex ground, and if you have had enough for one day, a rough descent westwards will return you to the quadbike path leading back to the start.

Otherwise, head north-west, taking care to avoid an arc of crags, partly surrounding the summit. The wide ridge gradually curves round to a north-east-

Lochboisdale from Beinn Ruigh Choinnich

Triuirebheann and Stulabhal from
Beinn Ruigh Choinnich

stream and climb easy grass slopes north-westwards, with a steep drop on the left down to Loch Stulabhal. Pass two small lochans higher up, before the terrain becomes steeper and craggier, leading to the trig point, standing on rocky ground, with a stupendously steep drop to the north down to lonely Loch Snigiscleit, circled by a girdle of smaller craggy peaks. The summit of Stulabhal feels wild and remote, with a totally different character to the previous two hills.

If ascending Stulabhal separately, the best route is from the north, at the Unasaraidh road end and via Trinneabhal and Airneabhal, and finally by Stulabhal's north-west ridge, probably its finest feature. A circuit could then be made round Loch Snigiscleit, over several other small, rocky summits. Alternatively, a shorter route begins from the track end at Loch nan Caorach, to the west.

To return, retrace steps to Bealach a' Chaolais and descend to Loch nan Arm, before rising to the col between Triuirebheinn and Cleit. Head south-west for 1km, to reach the quadbike path and follow it back to the start.

erly direction, descending to a broad col above Loch nan Arm on the left. From here, make a descending traverse into Bealach a' Chaolais, passing a ruin and the site of a souterrain, an Iron Age underground 'earth house', from the French '*sous terrain*' (under ground). This long bealach also contains the remains of several chambered cairns which are worth checking out.

From Bealach a' Chaolais, cross the

61. THACLA (HECLA) (606M/1,988FT)
62. BEINN CHORADAIL (527M/1,729FT)

MAP	OS SHEET 22 (GR 825345, 819329)
DISTANCE	18KM
ASCENT	850M
TIME	8–10 HRS
ACCESS	CAR PARK AT LOCH SGIOPORT ROAD END (B890) (GR 828386)
DIFFICULTY	A LONG AND SERIOUS EXPEDITION, OVER ESSENTIALLY PATHLESS, TUSSOCKY AND BOGGY TERRAIN, BUT INTERSPERSED WITH POCKETS OF ROUGH GNEISS
SUMMARY	A challenging, but satisfying, walk to two of the highest summits in South Uist. The walk could be extended to include the highest peak of Beinn Mhòr (620m) and this, with other options, are described in the main text.

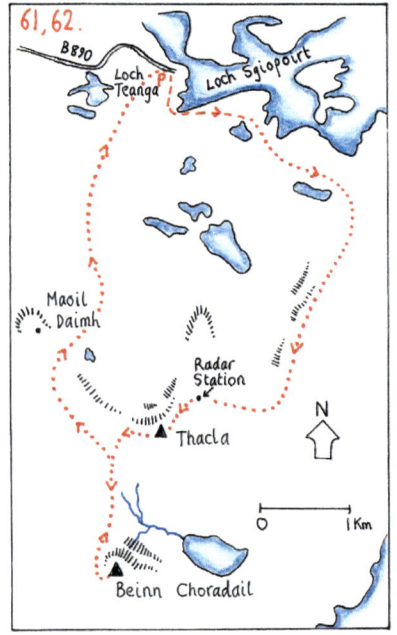

THE NAME HECLA and its modern Gaelic name of Thacla are likely derived from Heklefjell mountain in north Norway, from the Norwegian 'hekle', meaning hackle or comb and Thacla's summit ridge is distinctly comb-like. Beinn Choradail was originally Feaveallach, but it is unclear why the name changed. The Gaelic 'corr' is a sharp, pointed summit which certainly applies to Beinn Choradail.

If it is intended to climb Beinn Mhòr in addition to the above two summits and only one car is available, then it would be best to begin on the main A865 road at GR 768347, just north of Loch Dobhrain, where a track heads east for 1km. This also serves as an alternative starting point for the two

Beinn Choradail from the bealach lochan

hills only and is marginally shorter in distance, though not as scenic as the route to be described.

At the end of the Loch Sgioport road is a very small parking area on the left, with space for about four cars maximum. A signposted path begins just before here, following the head of the sea loch past some old shielings. Unfortunately, the path soon deteriorates into a boggy morass, and the wisest option is to stick to higher ground, making a beeline for the foot of Thacla's long, knobbly north ridge, to the east of Loch Bein and north of Maol Martaig. Once established on this broad ridge, the route is obvious and the terrain generally drier and more amenable to rhythmic walking. The ridge is a succession of craggy climbs and flat, grassy shoulders, eventually leading to the well-disguised radar station at Point 564, west of Beinn Sgalabhat. A short descent to a col, followed by an easy upward plod, lead to the rocky and airy summit of Thacla, a wonderful viewpoint. Sea eagles are very common in this area and if you haven't spotted one yet, there is still much of the day to go.

The second summit of Beinn Chora-

Thacla from Beinn Choradail

Thacla and Beinn Choradail from Beinn Mhor

dail is well seen from here, its actual top girdled by a steep band of crags, which can thankfully be breached on the south side. To descend to the col between the two peaks, it is advised to head west, following Thacla's comb-like, rocky ridge, which flattens out in a few hundred metres. From here, descend grassy slopes to the wide bealach, containing a small lochan from where Beinn Choradail looks particularly craggy and intimidating, its north-eastern face a wall of unbroken rock. Tend rightwards as you

climb on steep grass, staying below the girdle of crags, until an obvious grassy ramp is followed on a faint path, to reach the south ridge of the hill. From here it is only a short climb to reach the small cairn at the summit. It is worth spending some time here just to savour the remote isolation of such a rarely climbed peak.

The return to the start is still a long and complex undertaking, even by the shortest route. The best option is to retrace steps to the col, before contouring north-west along Thacla's southern slopes to reach the wide boggy col below Maoil Daimh. From here, an awkward, steep descent leads to more level ground, north of Loch a' Choire. Despite being only 2 miles (as the crow flies) to the starting point, the nature of the terrain, with its tussocks, hummocks, lochans and hidden trenches, will entail a walking speed of not much in excess of 1 mile per hour. Navigation can be simplified by heading to the right of Beinn Tairbeirt, the obvious hill north of the B890. Reach the road east of Loch Teanga and follow it to the starting point.

BENBECULA

63. RUABHAL FROM THE NORSE '*RU*', MEANING 'STREAM', OR POSSIBLY RED HILL (124M/407FT)

MAP	OS SHEET 22
DISTANCE	4KM
ASCENT	100M
TIME	1–2 HRS
ACCESS	MINOR ROAD END, WEST OF HILL (GR 811535)
DIFFICULTY	A SHORT AND STRAIGHTFORWARD WALK, FOLLOWING PART OF THE HEBRIDEAN WAY
SUMMARY	A perfect hill to climb on a summer evening, giving excellent panoramic vistas of the surrounding watery terrain.

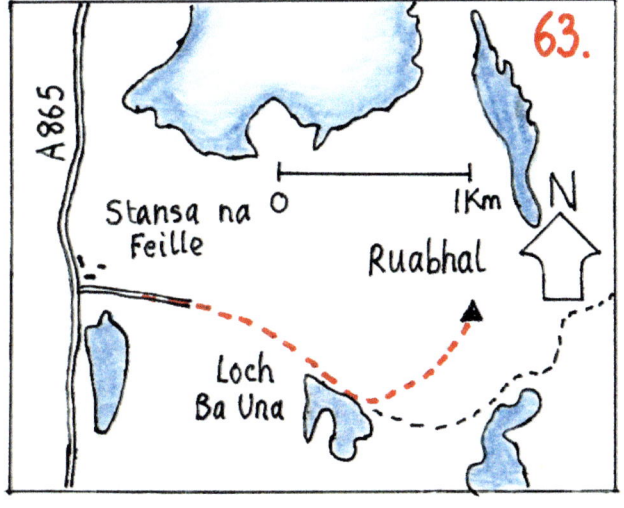

from almost anywhere on the island. It is a popular hill with both locals and tourists; more so with the recently formed Hebridean Way traversing its summit.

The route described is the shortest 'there and back' outing but could

AT A MODEST 124m above sea level, Ruabhal is the highest point of the water-laden, low-lying island of Benbecula. It stands in proud isolation, and as such, is a prominent landmark easily be lengthened to a circular trip with some unavoidable road walking. This is briefly outlined at the end.

Take the minor road leading east from the A865 just south of Stansa na

The summit of Ruabhal looking to Eabhal

Feille (market stance), and park on the left, near the island's recycling/landfill site. From here, walk along the obvious track eastward, over a cattle grid, following a line of wooden Hebridean Way marker posts. The track soon becomes a path passing Loch Ba' Una on the right. Fork left here and follow the marker posts up the hill on a less obvious path, sometimes boggy after rain. Higher up, the ground is drier and rockier and soon leads to the summit triangulation pillar and small cairn.

The summit panorama is absolutely breathtaking for such a small hill. This is an ideal spot to appreciate the myriad blue lochans covering the whole of Benbecula, with scores of tiny white cottages sprinkled like sugar grains on a green carpet. The view to the north-east is dominated by the long whaleback of Eabhal in North Uist (see following route).

Return by the ascent route or, alternatively, follow the marker posts northwards, down the gently sloping ridge between Dubh Loch and Loch Olabhat, to reach a minor road in 2km. Turn left and left again at the junction to reach the minor approach road in about 3km.

64. EABHAL (EAVAL) (347M/1,139FT)

MAP	OS SHEET 22 (GR 899605)
DISTANCE	12KM
ASCENT	350M
TIME	5–7 HRS
ACCESS	CAR PARK AT LOCH EUPHORT ROAD END (B894) (GR 891631)
DIFFICULTY	REASONABLE PATH FOR MUCH OF THE APPROACH, THOUGH BOGGY IN PLACES
SUMMARY	Eabhal is the highest hill in North Uist and its distinctive profile is obvious from numerous vantage points. Its ascent is arguably one of the best walks in the Uists, particularly for extensive views of a unique watery landscape.

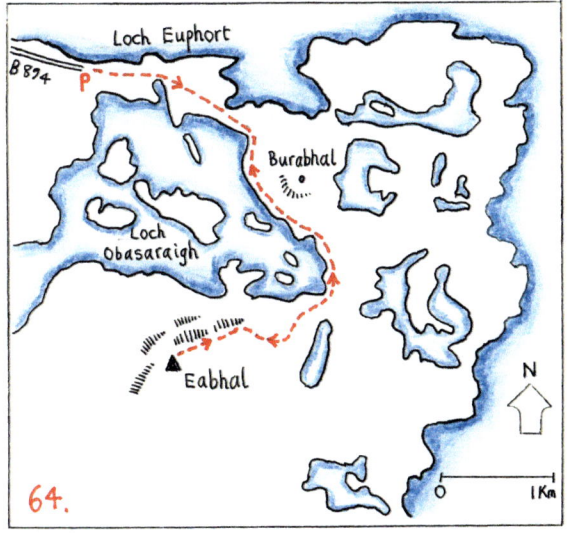

Norse '*ey fjall*', meaning island fell, a notion well appreciated from a glance at the OS map, showing the hill to be almost entirely surrounded by water; Loch Obasaraigh to the north and west and the Minch east and south.

There are a couple of points to note before beginning the main route description. Firstly, the start of the route is annoyingly just off of OS map 22, on the edge of OS map 18 –

THE NAME EABHAL (or Eaval on older maps) most likely originates from the

Eabhal from Loch Obasaraigh

though those using mobile phones for navigation will not be worried about such trivialities. Secondly, near the beginning of the walk, it is necessary to cross stepping stones at some tidal narrows and it is worth checking the tides before commencing the walk, though the stones only become submerged in very high tides.

Park at the car park at the end of the B894 next to the Beacon Studio and follow the track heading east through a gate and across grassy pasture. The path passes a small bay with the remains of a stone pier and continues across boggy ground to the stepping stones at GR 898631. These are fairly easy to cross when dry, but care should be taken when wet and/or wobbly! Beyond the stones, the path becomes very sketchy, with several boggy trenches providing interest. Cross a fence, below the imposing bulk of Burabhal, another smaller, craggy hill, which could also be climbed en route to Eabhal. The route now follows the edge of Loch Obasaraigh, skirting round the base of Burabhal on a sometimes muddy, but fairly distinct path. Across the loch, Eabhal rises in splendid isolation, in tiers

The author on Eabhal
(Photo: Andrew Oldfield)

of Lewisian gneiss and its easy-angled east ridge provides the obvious ascent route.

Reach an idyllic sandy beach at the head of the loch, an ideal spot for a breather and to check out the route ahead. The path continues intermittently but becomes more obvious at the foot of Eabhal. Initially the route swings to the east, avoiding crags and ascends steep grass and heathery gullies, to reach the broad shoulder of the east ridge. The remainder of the ascent is a tantalising mix of long outcropping gneiss slabs and long tongues of grass and heather. Plenty of scrambling opportunities are available for those of a more adventurous disposition.

The flat summit is surmounted by a stone triangulation pillar, circled by a stone shelter, and is a magnificent viewpoint for the surrounding panoramic jigsaw of land and water. This is an ideal vantage point for appreciating the amazing water-dominated landscape of North Uist. Return by the same route.

65. LÌ A TUATH NORTH LEE (263M/863FT)

MAP	OS SHEET 18 (GR 927660)
DISTANCE	10KM
ASCENT	285M
TIME	4–5 HRS
ACCESS	LAY-BY/PARKING AREA ON A867 (GR 896680)
DIFFICULTY	RELATIVELY EASY WALKING, BUT VERY BOGGY IN PLACES; A LINE OF POSTS MARKS ALL OF THE ROUTE
SUMMARY	An excellent short walk to occupy a half day, with exceptional panoramic views from a delightful rocky summit.

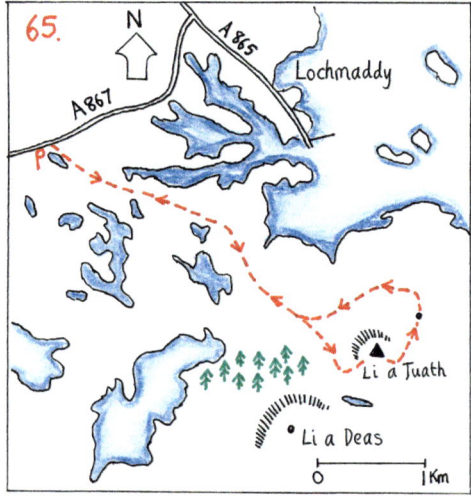

THE TWIN SUMMITS of Lì a Tuath and Lì a Deas, (North Lee and South Lee) are prominent landmarks to the south of Lochmaddy. Though North Lee is some 20m lower than South Lee, it is the shapeliest of the pair and has a marked route to its summit. The walk could easily be extended to include South Lee, which would add another 2km to the distance. This is described briefly in the text.

The parking area on the A867 road is clearly marked with a conspicuous yellow sign saying 'North Lee Walk', though the distance information of 10 miles is in error and should be 10km as above. Cross a small footbridge and stile, passing to the left of a lochan and follow the yellow-topped posts as they descend to cross a fence at another stile. From here, the route gains elevation, but is extremely boggy in places, as it weaves its way across the moor, with a sea inlet soon appearing on the left. Cross another small bridge and gradual-

Lì a Tuath and Li a Deas from Lochmaddy

ly move to the right of a fence as it goes uphill. North Lee is very prominent from here, rising up in tiers of gneiss.

If you intend to climb South Lee also, it is advised to leave the marked route at this point and trend right to reach the small reservoir nestling between the two hills. The summit is easily reached from the head of the reservoir in 180m of ascent, on grass and rock slabs. Return by the same way to rejoin the original marked route, which soon reaches the top of North Lee, its small cairn perched on a rocky crag. Take time to appreciate the marvellous summit views of the watery landscape to the west and Lochmaddy to the north.

From the summit, follow the marker posts as they descend eastwards initially, before turning north to arrive on the hill's subsidiary summit, crowned with a trig point. This is a better viewpoint for Lochmaddy and its island-studded harbour. Descend north from here, again following the marker posts, before swinging north-west to the position where a US Air Force plane crashed in

Start of the North Lee (Lì a Tuath) walk

A misty day on North Lee

1943, killing all 10 crew members. A small memorial marks the spot.

The posts gradually turn to head in a westerly direction, across the lower slopes and moor, to rejoin the ascent route at the fence. Follow the approach route for the last 3km back to the start.

GETTING TO THE UISTS

There is a CalMac ferry from Oban to Lochboisdale (South Uist) and also from Oban to Lochmaddy (North Uist). There is also a CalMac ferry from Uig on Skye to Lochmaddy. See CalMac website for details. There are also flights from various UK airports to Benbecula with Loganair being a key operator. See Loganair website for details.

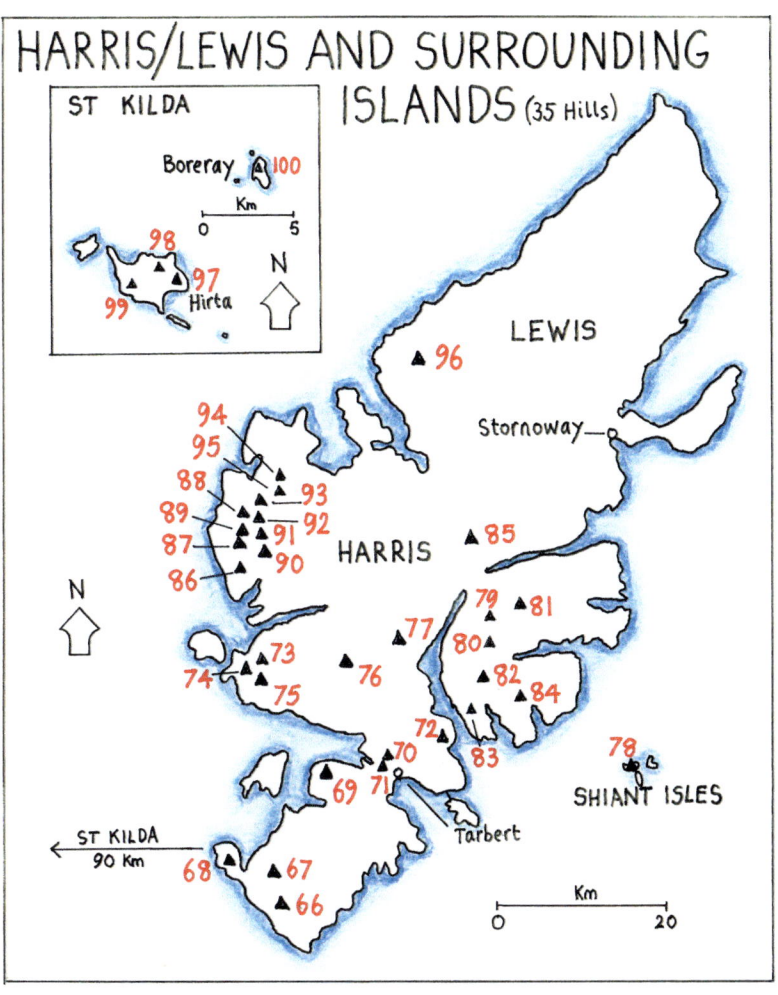

Boreray from Hirta (St Kilda)

SOUTH HARRIS

66. ROINEABHAL POINTED HILL / NORSE: ROUGH HILL (460M/1,508FT)

MAP	OS SHEET 18 (GR 043861)
DISTANCE	7KM
ASCENT	480M
TIME	3–4 HRS
ACCESS	GR 063854
DIFFICULTY	PATHLESS, ROUGH AND ROCKY; STEEP IN PLACES
SUMMARY	Roineabhal is the highest hill in South Harris, with a marvellous wild character and magnificent summit views.

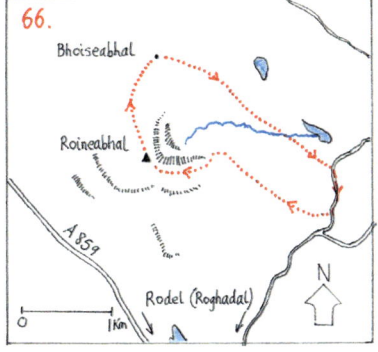

ROINEABHAL HAS MANY attributes usually associated with much higher mountains. In particular, it possesses a beautifully remote and steep-sided northern corrie, rarely visited, or indeed seen, by the casual pedestrian. Its topography is also more complex than many hills of similar height and the hill offers a variety of possible routes. Standing directly north of Rodel, most ascents are generally made from this vicinity. However, the described route begins at the high point on the minor road to Finsbay, giving the opportunity to view the northern corrie at close quarters, as well as involving less climbing and being a satisfying circular route.

The start of the route is about 3km from Rodel, on the high point of the road to Finsbay, which is east of Roineabhal. Ascend the broad ridge, west of the road, on heather and rocky outcrops, over a rise and down to a wee col. Ahead, is the steep ridge of Tora-cleit, forming the north-eastern boundary of Roineabhal's northern corrie.

Move right, avoiding any rock outcrops, to soon become established on the ridge, before making a direct ascent on steep heather and rock, but no real difficulty. The summit lies across the corrie, to the west. Gain height quickly, to reach the flat, stony top of Beinn na h-Aire, 'the hill of the look-out', with its

Leverburgh from Roineabhal

prominent cairn. This top is the south-east subsidiary summit of Roineabhal and it is only a short ridge walk to the main summit, with its triangulation pillar, surrounded by a ringed cairn.

As expected, the summit panorama is truly breathtaking, especially north-westwards, across the scattered township of Leverburgh to Ensay, Killegray and Pabbay and a profusion of smaller islets. The conical top of Ceapabhal (see Route 68) is very prominent, beyond the smaller hill of Greabhal.

Traverse the hill by continuing north, down rocky, but easy, slopes, which gradually broaden and flatten out at the col before Bhoiseabhal, Roineabhal's northern satellite top. A short ascent of about 70m leads to the summit.

Bhoiseabhal's obvious north-west ridge of Beinn Tharsuinn provides another possible ascent route to Roineabhal.

Descend from Bhoiseabhal, by its broad south-eastern ridge, giving grandstand views of Roineabhal's northern corrie. Although much of the rock is reportedly loose, there is an obvious, slabby buttress on the right-hand side of the corrie, which could repay further exploration – at least that's what I wrote in my log after I had completed this route!

At the base of the ridge, cross a small stream and contour along the foot of the ridge traversed at the start of the route. Reach the road in less than half a kilometre, from where it is only a similar distance to your starting point.

67. BLEABHAL BUTTER HILL (398M/1,305FT)

MAP	OS SHEET 18 (GR 031915)
DISTANCE	7KM
ASCENT	350M
TIME	3–4 HRS
ACCESS	GR 045890 (LOCH LANGAVAT)
DIFFICULTY	ROUGH, TUSSOCKY AND PATHLESS
SUMMARY	A fine circular route, to a shapely summit with excellent views.

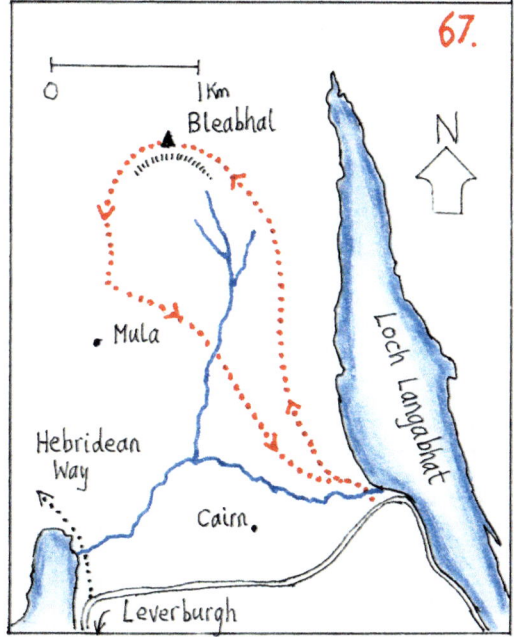

BLEABHAL IS THE highest of a group of lower hills, standing north of Leverburgh and south of Borve. It is also the one possessing most character, with a beautiful south facing corrie, enclosed by gentle ridges, providing ideal ascent and descent routes. The described route, therefore, begins south of the hill, at the point where the minor road swings right to Loch Langavat. Note that the hill can be accessed from the A859 Leverburgh to Tarbert road, to the north, involving a roughly similar distance, but is not as aesthetically appealing. The more adventurous may well wish to complete a circuit of all the hills in the group, and a suitable starting point for this would be the east side of Loch na Moracha, where the long-distance route, The Hebridean Way, leaves the minor road (GR 024884).

Taransay and Harris from Bleabhal

Park at a suitable point, and begin the walk by descending slightly to cross the Abhainn an Uisge, which strangely translates as 'river of water'! It is, thankfully, more of a small stream than a river. Head north-west initially, then north, keeping to the high ground of a low, tussocky ridge – Druim nan Caorach. In less than 2km, the ridge becomes significantly steeper, and gradually curves westward, giving a fine ascent on springy turf and small outcrops to a stony summit, with trig pillar and wee cairn.

The summit panorama is stunning and a uniquely Hebridean blend of turquoise sea, sandy strands, islands and hills, all, hopefully, under a blue and cloud-flecked sky.

The descent follows the line of the ridge forming the western boundary of the big, grassy corrie, south of the summit, which gradually leads down to a broad bealach, where you descend south-eastwards to Gleann a' Chaimire. Cross a small stream and contour round the lower slopes of Druim nan Caorach for 1km to return to the road and point of departure.

68. CEAPABHAL CAP-SHAPED HILL; OR BOW-SHAPED HILL IN NORSE (368M/1,207FT)

MAP	OS SHEET 18 (GR 973924)
DISTANCE	13KM
ASCENT	470M
TIME	4–6 HRS
ACCESS	MACGILLIVRAY CENTRE, NORTHTON (TAOBH TUATH)
DIFFICULTY	MOSTLY PATHLESS, ROUGH WALKING, WITH A STEEP ASCENT AND BOGGY SECTIONS
SUMMARY	Ceapabhal rises in isolated splendour, on its own little peninsula, and its ascent, followed by a fine coastal walk, is one of the classic outings in South Harris.

THE TOE HEAD peninsula is almost a separate island from Harris and is essentially one prominent and shapely hill, standing high above the golden sands of Scarasta beach. The described route visits an ancient chapel on the west coast, before traversing the hill and returning by the north and east coast, passing several natural rock arches.

From the A859 Leverburgh road, take the minor road to Northton (or Taobh Tuath) and park at the MacGillivray Centre, near the road end. Walk to the road end and its continuation along a sandy track for almost a 1km to a gate, where several paths radiate outwards. Follow the leftmost track across glorious machair. Machair is lush pasture, formed by the wind blowing fine shell sand onto boggy, acidic grassland, resulting in a profusion of wild flowers in spring and early summer.

The track then hugs the coastline between several idyllic little sandy coves and the lower slopes of Ceapabhal on your right. You soon reach a picturesque, ruined chapel – Rubh' an Teampaill (temple on the promontory), built

Traigh Scarasta from Ceapabhal

in the 16th century. A plaque nearby gives more information.

Ceapabhal can be ascended directly from the chapel, but it is easier to return along the path for half a kilometre, before tackling the steep slopes forming the south-east ridge of the hill. You will need to cross a drystone wall en route. Once established on the ridge, head directly upwards, through a maze of rock and deep heather, and enjoy increasingly magnificent views in all directions.

The tough little climb levels out to tussocky moorland, crowned by a trig point and cairn, where a well-earned rest is in order. On a clear day, the summit panorama is simply stunning. The wide expanse of the Scarasta sands is spread out to the east, while further north lies the island of Taransay, used in the BBC television series *Castaway* 2000. In addition to the multitude of smaller islets, peppering the Sound of Harris, the un-mistakable profile of the St Kilda group often appear as stubby brush strokes, some 70km west, on a distant horizon.

Descend north-west to a col and continue over a minor top (339m), before a long, gradual descent down the hill's north-west ridge on grass and rock terraces takes you to a wee lochan, with a hillock beyond, marking the point of Toe Head. This is a beautifully wild and remote spot and is the start of a wonderful clockwise coastal walk back to the outward track.

There is a natural arch at Toe Head itself, but look out for another at GR 966946, which is very close to the land behind it, and the water visible through the narrow gap has the appearance of a blowhole. The going can be quite tiresome in places and you will have to cross several fences via gates. Look out for Highland cattle. From Toe Head, it is about 6km back to the outward track across the machair.

69. BEINN DHUBH BLACK HILL (506M/1,661FT)

MAP	OS SHEET 14 (GR 089007)
DISTANCE	11KM
ASCENT	540M
TIME	4–5 HRS
ACCESS	GR 095974
DIFFICULTY	AN EASY BUT PATHLESS HILLWALK
SUMMARY	A beautiful circular walk, to arguably the finest viewpoint in South Harris.

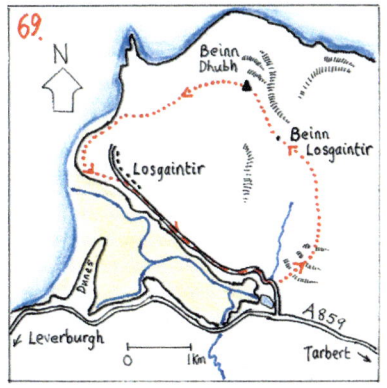

BEINN DHUBH IS the highest point and western culmination of a long ridge of hills from Uabhal Mor in the south-east. The entire ridge, including Uabhal Mor and Ceann Reamhar, would be a fine expedition for the more energetic, but the described route is slightly less ambitious. Beinn Dhubh is very conspicuous from the Leverburgh to Tarbert road, looking across Traigh Losgaintir (Luskentyre Sands), a classic photographic viewpoint.

Take the minor road to Losgaintir for only a few hundred metres and park at or near the bridge over the Allt Tobhtan ic Fannan. Go through a kissing gate and cross the stream on steppingstones to reach the base of Sròn Godamuil, a slabby spur forming your ascent route. Climb up a succession of delightfully rough rock slabs and grassy tongues, with optional scrambling if so inclined.

At a height of about 250m, the spur levels off and you pass a small lochan, before again rising on easier ground, to reach the main ridge, at a height of just over 400m. Veer left and traverse the subsidiary top of Beinn Losgaintir, before descending slightly to a stony bealach. Climb the last 100m to the summit trig point of Beinn Dhubh.

The views in all directions are superb, but particularly to the north and west. Across West Loch Tarbert, looking north, the higher hills of North Harris

Beinn Dhubh from Luskentyre

are lined up in a complex array of ridges, spurs and corries, while the view west is dominated by the golden sands of Tràigh Rosamol and the island of Taransay, set like a jewel in a turquoise sea.

Traverse the hill by descending directly west, aiming for the south-western extremity of Aird Grodanais, the obvious promontory projecting into the Sound of Taransay. Pass through a gate in a fence and another gate in the drystone wall above Tràigh Rosamol and follow the sands round to Losgaintir, from where the minor road leads back to the start in about 3km.

Taransay from Beinn Dhubh

The view southwest from Beinn Dhubh

NORTH HARRIS

70. SGAOTH AIRD HIGH WING (559M/1,834FT)
71. GIOLABHAL GLAS GILLI'S FELL (475M/1,558FT)

MAP	OS SHEET 14 (GR 166040, 149023)
DISTANCE	11KM
ASCENT	900M
TIME	5–6 HRS
ACCESS	PARKING AREA AT START OF HUSINIS ROAD (B887) (GR 137035)
DIFFICULTY	ESSENTIALLY PATHLESS WALKING WITH A 'HIGH MOUNTAIN FEEL'
SUMMARY	The part horseshoe route described is a satisfying undertaking, giving unrivalled views of the An Cliseam group and other surrounding peaks.

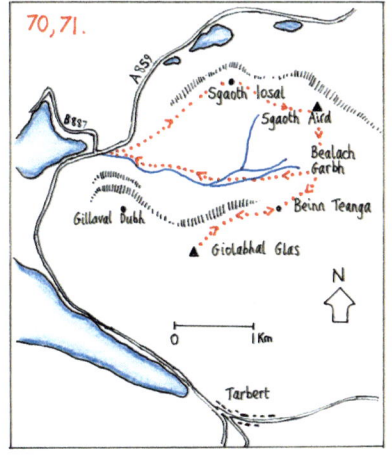

THESE TWO HILLS are the highest of several, forming a compact horseshoe, directly north of Tarbert. The main corrie, holding the Skeaudale River and the 'open' end of the horseshoe, face directly west and it is from the west that the walk begins. A glance at the map would suggest that a complete circuit of the horseshoe is a viable option, but it should be noted that the northern and western slopes of Gillaval Dubh (forming the southern termination of the horseshoe) are extremely steep, with sheer crags and awkward rock bands. Several accidents, including at least one fatality, have occurred involving attempted descents of this peak. For this reason, the clockwise circuit described, backtracks eastward from the second hill of Giolabhal Glas, before returning from Bealach Garbh down the easy corrie.

The start is at the beginning of the B887 Huisinis road, which leaves the main A859 Tarbert to Stornoway road 5km north of Tarbert. There is a substantial parking area on the immediate left, overlooking the bay. Cross the A859

The An Cliseam group from Sgaoth Aird

and follow the road north for about 100m, before branching off right to begin ascending the south-western slopes of Sgaoth Iosal, the first peak of the round. The gentle angle of ascent gradually increases as you climb and you will need to negotiate some slabby bands of rock higher up, presenting no insurmountable problems. Beyond here, the angle eases considerably and it is a gentle plod to the wee summit of Sgaoth Iosal. Enjoy cracking views north to Harris's only Corbett of An Cliseam and its satellite summits.

Sgaoth Aird, the first main hill, lies only 1km further on and involves losing height for about 80m, before a 100m ascent on grass and slabs brings you to the flat, spacious summit, crowned by a ringed shelter cairn surrounding an inner cairn. This is a phenomenal viewpoint of not only An Cliseam, but Todun and Caiteseal, with the Shiant Islands in the far west. Your second summit of Giolabhal Glas is also visible across the corrie to the south-west.

From the summit, head directly south, down very easy grass slopes for just under 1km and 150m of height loss, to reach the broad col of Bealach Garbh. This is the start of the main descent route into the huge west-facing corrie on your right. It will take around

The lochan below the summit of Giolabhal Glas

2 hours to complete the return journey from here to Giolabhal Glas.

From Bealach Garbh, ascend grassy slopes south-westwards, aiming for the intermediate top of Beinn na Teanga. From here, there is a quite steep descent of 100m, though bands of small crags, with the easiest line to the right. The final ascent to Giolabhal Glas is a thoroughly pleasant, gentle plod on grass and slabs, passing a small lochan, giving excellent photo opportunities. The summit area of the hill has three distinct cairns, the middle one being the highest and the most southerly one the largest, with a trig point, and giving excellent views down to the village of Tarbert and the Isle of Scalpay.

Do not attempt to descend this hill any other way than retracing steps to Bealach Garbh. Easy slopes do exist south from Beinn na Teanga, but this takes you to Tarbert and not the starting point. Despite the absence of a path, the long, leisurely descent into the western corrie from Bealach Garbh is a delightful way to end the walk. Underfoot, the terrain is gentle and grassy and the only interruptions to the rhythm are the crossing of a couple of stream gorges. Reach the road in 2.5km to complete the route.

72. TODUN ORIGIN OBSCURE (528M/ 1,733FT)

MAP	OS SHEET 14 (GR 210030)
DISTANCE	14 KM
ASCENT	850M
TIME	6–8 HRS
ACCESS	LOCHANNAN LACASDAIL CAR PARK (GR 184005)
DIFFICULTY	A CHALLENGING AND RELATIVELY SERIOUS WALK, THOUGH MUCH OF IT ON GOOD PATHS
SUMMARY	A stunning circuit, full of interest, initially along a spectacular old footpath, followed by the highlight of the day – a steep ascent of Todun.

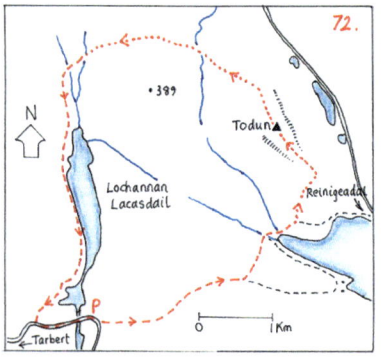

TODUN PRESENTS A steep, fin-like profile from some aspects and a sharp pyramid from others; almost like a smaller version of Schiehallion. It is a relatively popular hill and is regularly climbed from the Reinigeadal youth hostel at its south-eastern foot.

The hamlet of Reinigeadal was created in the 1820s by folk from the west side of Harris, who were forced to leave their good land for sheep. The only access

to the village for over 160 years was by boat, or the walking route which forms the initial part of this walk. In 1989 a new road was finally built to this isolated little outpost and provides the quickest means of ascent of Todun. However, this does the hill little justice and misses out the finest footpath on Harris.

Park at the car park just beyond the bridge at the southern end of Lochannan Lacasdail (Laxadale lochs). This is only 3km from Tarbert, on the road to Scalpay. From the parking area take the footpath, signposted Reinigeadal, which climbs gradually over heather moor, to reach a large cairn at a wide saddle between two hills. From here, there is a dramatic view of the Shiant Islands (see Route 78) and if it is a clear day, possibly the Scottish mainland.

From this high point at the col, the path descends in a series of spectacular

A distant view of Todun

Todun from the Reinigeadal path

zigzags, to lonely Loch Trolamaraig, a sheltered sea inlet. For those with un-limited time, there is the option of leaving the main path just beyond the col and turning right along another path, leading to the abandoned village of Moilingeanais. A return path contours along the shoreline to reach the main path at the head of Loch Trolamaraig. This loop is about 3km and would add at least another hour to the above time.

From the head of the sea inlet, continue along the path, crossing two bridges, and climb up to a flattish area containing a mass of barrel-shaped, ice-scoured, gneiss slabs. This is the point to leave the path and begin the ascent to the prominent south-east ridge of Todun. Gaining the crest of the ridge involves the crossing of a large gully, formed by the Allt Dubh, then climbing up to the right on fairly steep, heathery ground, avoiding any crags, to reach the narrow crest of the ridge. This initial section can seem quite intimidating, but by the easiest line is just a steep slog.

Once on the ridge crest, follow a fairly well-defined path through heather and rock outcrops to the summit trig point, a grand spot for rest and refreshments and to admire the wide-ranging views. Descend the much broader north ridge for just over 1km, before gradually veering off left into a wide depression, to cross a burn. Contour easily round to reach an expansive, flat area, north of the minor peak of Strathabhal. Head west, passing a tiny lochan, surrounded by knolls, before finally descending steep, heathery slopes for a short distance, to reach the good footpath north of Lochannan Lacasdail.

Turn left and follow the path round a big bend, reaching the loch in 1km. The undemanding walk along the west bank of the loch is a pleasure, after the previous rough, cross-country section. Finally, reach the road and turn left to return to the parking area. This completes a satisfying circuit.

73. CEARTABHAL UPRIGHT HILL? (556M/1,824FT)
74. HUISEABHAL MÒR BIG HOUSE HILL (489M/1,603FT)
75. LEOSABHAL ORIGIN UNCERTAIN (412M/1,352FT)

MAP	OS SHEET 13 (GR 043127, 023117, 038099)
DISTANCE	16KM
ASCENT	850M
TIME	6–8 HRS
ACCESS	GLEANN CHLIOSTAIR (GR 055082)
DIFFICULTY	REASONABLE APPROACH PATH – OTHERWISE, PATHLESS, GRASSY HILLWALKING
SUMMARY	These three hills in West Harris provide a marvellous day's hillwalking in delectable surroundings, with ever-changing views. Ceartabhal could be climbed from Huisinis as a separate trip and this option is briefly described.

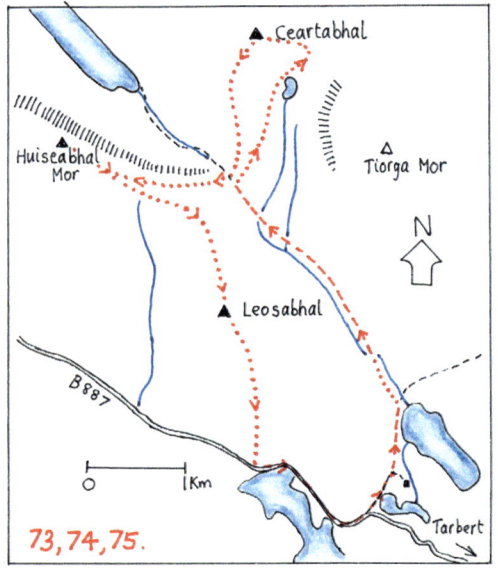

THE SINGLE-TRACK ROAD to the tiny coastal hamlet of Huisinis is one of the most scenic drives on Harris, with a mountain wilderness to its north for the entire journey. Two main glens run northwards from this road: Gleann Mhiabhaig and Gleann Chliostair, providing access to this unique area.

The entrance to Gleann Chliostair lies some 13km along the B887 and there is usually room to park 400m up the glen road at the right-hand turn off for the fish hatchery. Walk up the track for 700m to a bridge, where the map indi-

Ceartabhal from Huiseabhal Mor

cates a path going up Gleann Leosaid on the left. This path is essentially non-existent until it crosses the stream further up the glen and should be visible rising up the hillside in the distance. Unfortunately, the initial pathless section is often boggy, but after a few hundred metres, cross the stream to reach the path proper, which is dry and well-constructed.

The next 2km give an easy, gradual ascent to the broad bealach between Ceartabhal to the north and Huiseabhal Mòr and Leosabhal to the south. The path itself continues north-west down to the steep-sided Glen Cravadale and provides a possible alternative ascent route from Huisinis. You may wish to ascend Ceartabhal on a separate trip by

this route.

Otherwise, turn right and ascend easy-angled grass slopes to the attractive Loch Bràigh Bheagarais, nestling serenely in the hollow below the steep, craggy west flank of Tiorga Mor (a Graham) on the right and the more friendly slopes of Ceartabhal on the left. Continue upwards to the col above, before turning left to climb the last 150m to the flat summit of Ceartabhal, a magnificent viewpoint, especially north over Loch Resort to the Uig hills beyond.

Descend south-west then south, avoiding any crags, to eventually reach the broad bealach and the ascent path. Pleasant grass slopes lead upwards on the opposite side for a height gain of around

Leosabhal from Huiseabhal Mor

250m to the equally flat summit of Huiseabhal Mòr. The finest feature of this
hill is its steep northern cliffs, dropping
dramatically into Glen Cravadale, which
you will have glimpsed on the ascent.

To the south-east lies the final hill
of Leosabhal and is easily reached by
descending broad, grassy slopes and
traversing the mini hill of Beidig, before
ascending Leosabhal's slabby, easy-angled north-west ridge to its prominent
summit cairn set on a massive boulder.
This is an ideal spot to rest and enjoy
more magnificent views, this time south,
across the bay, to Taransay and the
white sands of South Harris.

The descent, south-eastward, is a
delight in dry weather, with a seemingly
endless succession of huge, rough boil-
er-plate gneiss slabs providing excellent
purchase, interspersed with grassy
ramps and runnels. Reach the road near
a house and turn left for just over 1km,
to the entrance to Gleann Chliostair
and your starting point.

The summit of Leosabhal

76. STULABHAL HILL OF THE SHIELING HUT – NORSE (579M/1,901FT)
77. LIUTHAID SEE TEXT (492M/1,615FT)

MAP	OS SHEET 13 OR 14 (GR 133122, 175136)
DISTANCE	18KM
ASCENT	1,230M
TIME	7–9 HRS
ACCESS	ABHAINN BHIOGADAIL CAR PARK (A859) (GR 187116)
DIFFICULTY	MAINLY ON EXCELLENT PATHS BUT MUCH ASCENT AND DESCENT
SUMMARY	The ascent of these two hills, but especially Stulabhal, takes the walker into wild and expansive mountainous terrain and is the haunt of golden eagles. Liuthaid, the less remote of the two, can easily be climbed as a separate excursion.

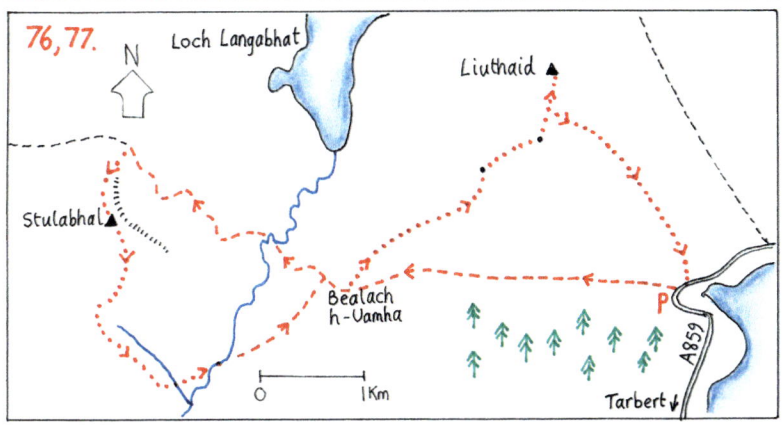

THE TANGLED, MOUNTAINOUS topography west of Loch Seaforth in North Harris is dominated by An Clisean, a Corbett, and the highest hill in the Outer Hebrides. The remaining hills comprise a handful of Grahams and a few gems under 2,000 feet, including these two, lying in the northern extremity of the area. Stulabhal is a wonderfully remote peak, seeing few visitors, whilst Liuthaid is readily accessible from the A859. The name Liuthaid, means 'several' or 'many' and possibly refers

Approaching Stulabhal

to the many tops on its summit ridge.

The access car park is at the bend in the road just north of the bridge and is the starting point for a very long walk to the golden eagle viewing centre in Gleann Mhiabhaig. This is normally accessed from the south, by a significantly shorter walk along the glen on a good track. The walk from here to the southern end of Gleann Mhiabhaig is one of the finest wilderness walks in Harris, if transport logistics can be solved.

The initial part of the walk is an ideal warm-up along an excellent path, making a gradual rising traverse of the southern flank of Liuthaid. You will notice that there has been much regeneration of native trees in the wide corrie

south of the path. An easy 3km leads to Bealach na h-Uamha (bealach of the cave), a narrow defile, marking the start up the ascent of Liuthaid on the return from Stulabhal.

Descend from the bealach on the other side, ignoring a path branching off to the left. This is relatively recent and unmarked on my own map, but provides a good return route from Stulabhal, now very prominent in the view ahead. After descending about 150m, cross the Abhainn Langadail on a new bridge and begin the straightforward ascent on the opposite side, on a good grassy path, zigzagging upwards for 2km and a 300m height gain, to reach the lonely col between Stulabhal and its northerly top of Rapaire.

The obvious spur on the left provides the final leg of the ascent, up its fairly steep and heathery slopes, avoiding any crags in the upper reaches. As the angle eases, swing round to the left to reach the cairn and trig point.

The view northeast from Stulabhal

The panoramic view from the summit is wilderness personified, the works of man totally absent. Southwards is a complex tangle of ridges and summits, while northwards, the long, convoluted arm of Loch Langabhat probes into a trackless terrain of myriad lochans and utter desolation.

Leave the summit in a south-easterly direction and descend the broad, grassy spur, gradually veering right to reach the wide bealach below Creag Stulabhal. Easy grass slopes then lead down to the wide glen and the Abhainn Langadail, which can be crossed carefully on a log, near a deer fence. Join the recently constructed path which makes a gradual, rising traverse to the outward path, just below the Bealach na h-Uamha.

The bealach is the start of the climb up Liuthaid, but if you have had enough for one day, then return by the outward track, east to the road and car park.

The initial climb to Liuthaid passes a tiny lochan, reaching a broad shoulder, before steeper slopes lead eventually to Mullach a' Ruisg (the 'bare summit') marked by a small cairn. A line of old fence posts lead across the broad ridge to the next top of Mullach Bhiogadail, and from here, an easy stroll takes you to the large cairn crowning the summit of Liuthaid, another excellent viewpoint.

The best descent route returns to the wide col between Liuthaid and Mullach Bhiogadail, before descending east, gradually veering south-east down easy-angled grass slopes, reaching the road slightly north of the start.

GETTING TO HARRIS

CalMac offer services including Uig to Tarbert (Harris) and Ullapool to Stornoway (Lewis). See CalMac website for details. Flights are also available to Stornoway from various Scottish airports. See Loganair website for details.

78. MULLACH BUIDHE YELLOW SUMMIT (160M/525FT)

MAP	OS SHEET 14 (GR 415987)
DISTANCE	2KM
ASCENT	240M
TIME	1–2 HRS
ACCESS	PEBBLE BEACH ISTHMUS (GR 418978) (SEE END FOR ISLAND ACCESS)
DIFFICULTY	AWKWARD, ROCKY TERRAIN INITIALLY, FOLLOWED BY STEEP 'GRASS SCRAMBLING', TRICKIER ON THE DESCENT
SUMMARY	Probably a once-in-a-lifetime ascent for many, a visit to the high point of the Shiants is a truly magical and out-of-this-world experience.

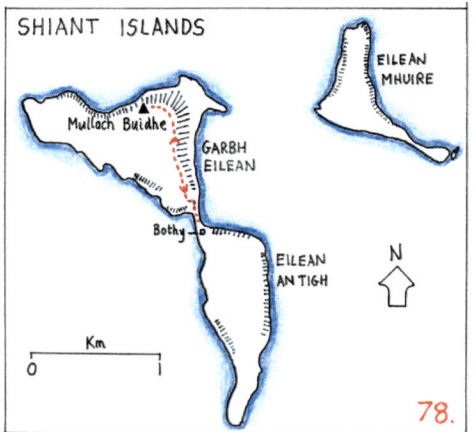

THE SHIANT ISLANDS are an archipelago of three small islands, two 'joined at the hip' by a narrow isthmus of pebble beach, which can become submerged in very high tides. The name 'Shiant Islands' is an anglicisation of *Na h-Eileanan Seunta*, translating roughly as 'Enchanted Isles'. The three island names of Garbh Eilean, Eilean an Taigh (or Tigh) and Eilean Mhuire, translate as Rough Island, House Island and Mary's Island respectively, the middle one containing a small house, or bothy, to be more accurate.

Geologically, the islands are an extension of Skye's Trotternish peninsula, and although closer to Lewis than Skye, the underlying rock is similar to Staffa, the Giant's Causeway in Antrim and Staffin in Skye. The dolerite and Tertiary basalt columns form spectacular cliffs, over 120m high on Garbh Eilean's north side, which formed around 60 million years ago, much younger than the ancient, weathered gneiss of Harris and Lewis.

The initial steep section of Mullach Buidhe from the beach

The islands have been owned by the Nicolson family since 1937, when Nigel Nicolson bought them and subsequently passed them on to his son Adam, author of what is generally considered to be the definitive book on the islands: *Sea Room*, published in 2001. In 2005, the Shiants were passed on to Adam's son Tom, who is the current owner.

The Shiants hold a significant bird population and are home to around 60,000 breeding pairs of puffins, with thousands of kittiwakes, guillemots, razorbills, and fulmars nesting on ledges among the huge fluted basalt columns on the cliffs of all three islands.

The normal landing time of 2 hours should provide adequate duration for the return trip to Mullach Buidhe, but probably little else for an average hill-walker. A thorough exploration of both connected islands will require at least two boat trips, but it should be noted that it is possible to book the bothy on Eilean an Taigh for an extended stay by contacting the islands' owner via the www.shiantisles.net website.

The standard landing point is east of the shingle isthmus between the two main islands and this provides the starting point for the ascent of Mullach Buidhe. A first glance up at Mullach

The beach and bothy from high on Mullach Buidhe

Buidhe's southern defensive bastion of Sron Lionta (full or bulbous nose), gives the impression of unrelenting steepness and is a hint intimidating, with the lowest rocks and cliffs seemingly having no noticeable breach in their defences. However, further right (east) of the shingle beach, a scattering of lighter-coloured rocks conceals a vague path which ascends upwards to the right, before doubling back left into a hidden gully, bringing you out onto grassy slopes above the line of lower cliffs.

From here, make a rising traverse leftwards to another steep, grassy gully and ascend this for about 20m to reach a path which contours along to the left for around 100m, before reaching a very obvious long, grassy gully stretching up to the right through a band of crags. Zigzag up this gully to eventually emerge on a flattish area, giving superb views down to the shingle beach and bothy. The angle eases considerably here; keep ascending over a small bump to reach the top of Sron Lionta.

The actual summit of Mullach Buidhe is now only 500m away and reaching it is best accomplished by following the cliff top rather than a direct route inland, which can be notoriously boggy. Enjoy glorious views down the vertiginous cliffs and across to Eilean Mhuire. In summer, when you are most likely

Eilean Mhuire from Mullach Buidhe

to be doing this walk, the cliff tops are awash with wild flowers, including bog cotton, asphodel and pimpernel, along with orchids, tormentil and milkwort. Look out also for puffin burrows and the odd arctic skua. The summit area is cairnless but reputedly had a trig point at one time, of which there are no discernible remains.

Return by the exact route of ascent, taking extreme care on the steep final descent. A wooden post that you would have passed on the way up makes a good guide on the way down. Hopefully there is time for a quick visit to the bothy before your boat departs.

GETTING TO THE SHIANT ISLANDS

Various boat tour operators offer half-day or full-day trips from either Stornoway or Tarbert. Isle of Harris Sea Tours (also known as Kilda Cruises) is one of the best and most well-known, operating from Tarbert. Their staff are very approachable, friendly and they offer a full tour of the islands with a 2-hour landing plus tea or coffee, cake and even a free dram! (www.isleofharrisseatours.com; Tel: 01859 502060). Check online for this and other operators.

LEWIS

79. GUAINEAMOL POSSIBLY HILL OF LIGHTNESS (406M/1,332FT)
80. MUAITHEABHAL ORIGIN OBSCURE (424M/1,391FT)
81. FEIRIOSBHAL ORIGIN OBSCURE (327M/1,073FT)

MAP	OS SHEET 14 (GR 262135, 258114, 301146)
DISTANCE	18KM
ASCENT	980M
TIME	7–9 HRS
ACCESS	BRIDGE ON EISHKEN ROAD (GR 298162)
DIFFICULTY	MAINLY PATHLESS, ROUGH WALKING IN A REMOTE AREA
SUMMARY	For lovers of wild, untamed landscapes, this demanding walk is a must. With the exception of Feiriosbhal, the hills are grassy and rounded but possess a serious and remote atmosphere.

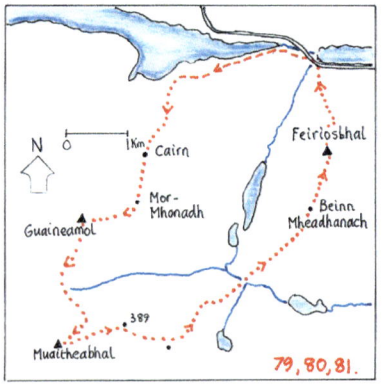

THE AREA OF south-east Lewis, known as Pairc (park), is essentially an almost inaccessible domain of lonely hills, lochs and glens, inhabited by golden eagles, sea eagles and red-throated divers. Lying east of the long, contorted arm of Loch Seaforth, the area is almost an island, and only a 6km stretch of river in the north prevents it from assuming this status.

Plans to erect a wind farm on the west side of Feiriosbhal appear to have stalled somewhat and it is hoped that this unique wilderness is retained as such. Due to its remoteness and lack of footpaths, the area sees few walkers and you are likely to meet no-one on these three hills. This walk is a good introduction to Pairc and could be shortened by excluding Muaitheabhal, which could easily be combined with an ascent of Beinn Mhòr, the highest hill in the area. (See Route 82, 83)

From the A859 Stornoway road, take the minor road to Eishken for 6km and park either before or beyond the bridge near Loch Sgiobacleit. Walk along the

The summit of Guaineamol

track heading west, below steep slopes on your left and the head of Loch Seaforth on your right. At the end of the track near a building, cross the burn and head south up gradually steepening slopes, on heather and grass, to eventually reach a cairn on the level ridge, north of Mor Mhonadh. (great moor). There is a distinct Cairngorm feeling as you stride out along this broad, grassy ridge to Mor Mhonadh. The ridge then veers west to the true summit of Guaineamol.

From this summit, descend southwest, then south, down easy grass slopes to a broad saddle at a height of 240m. The next summit of Muaitheabhal can be tackled directly, or by making a rising traverse to the left, before ascending gradual slopes to the small cairn marking the summit. The top feels like a long way from anywhere and although Beinn Mhòr seems just a hop away to the south, it is better left for another day.

From the summit, head initially to the wide saddle, before Beinn na h-Uamha,

The view west from Muaitheabhal

Feiriosbhal and Loch Airigh Thormaid

and either traverse this hill, or skirt south round its summit to another col. Turn north-east here, to descend an obvious stony spur, in the exact direction of Feiriosbhal. At the end of this spur there are sheer crags, which are avoided by dropping down steep grassy slopes to the right.

Cross a stream, to reach the expansive lower slopes of Beinn Mheadhanach, the southern outlier of Feiriosbhal, and make a long, gradual ascent to this rocky little summit. The final stretch to Feiriosbhal is a pleasant meander along a broad ridge, containing knolls and tiny lochans, before a short, steep climb to the trig point, a marvellous viewpoint. Of the three hills,

this one has by far the finest character.

Continue northwards along the ridge and descend to a grassy shoulder, before Creag na h-Uamha. Now descend north-west on fairly steep grass and heather slopes, to reach the road in 1km. Turn left to reach your starting point and complete a satisfying round.

The view south from Feiriosbhal

82. BEINN MHÒR BIG HILL (572M/1,877FT)
83. CAITESEAL ORIGIN UNCERTAIN (449M/1,473FT)

MAP	OS SHEET 13 OR 14 (GR 254096, 242044)
DISTANCE	18KM (FROM WILDCAMP – SEE TEXT)
ASCENT	1,020M
TIME	8–10 HRS
ACCESS	EISGEIN (SPELT EISHKEN ON SOME MAPS) ROAD END (GR 325119 OR 325123)
DIFFICULTY	TOTALLY PATHLESS AND AWKWARD TERRAIN, RANGING FROM BOG AND TUSSOCKS TO BARE ROCK AND DEEP HEATHER, WITH MUCH ASCENT AND DESCENT; THIS IS A DEMANDING AND COMMITTING HIKE INCLUDING THE REMOTEST HILL IN THIS BOOK (THE APPROACH TO THE WILDCAMP IS MAINLY ON GOOD PATHS)
SUMMARY	An exacting, but varied tramp connecting the highest peak in Lewis's Pairc district and the most remote – a truly memorable outing, best attempted in favourable weather conditions.

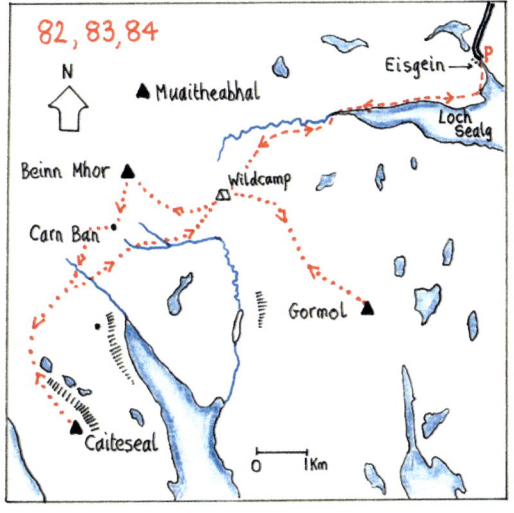

THESE TWO HILLS and the following one (Gormol) are situated in the southern part of the Pairc district and are easily the remotest summits described in this book. Only one lonely road leads to the periphery of this desolate, but hauntingly beautiful region, at the tiny hamlet of Eisgein on the north side of Loch Sealg, a sea loch. It is only relatively recently that the last 6km of the route to Eisgein was

The summit of Beinn Mhòr

upgraded to a single-track tarmac road.

Beinn Mhòr and Gormol can both be ascended directly from Eisgein, or from a wild camp situated between the two peaks. The real reason for this camp, however, is to access the second hill in this route description, namely Caiteseal, one of the most inaccessible summits in the whole of the UK, and a prized objective for the discerning hillwalker. The recommended camp spot is just north of a small lochan at GR 274092, and two nights here allow these two hills and Gormol to be comfortably ascended. This was the strategy used by the author. Gormol can be climbed

either on the first or third day, and the long middle day used for Beinn Mhòr and Caiteseal.

At this juncture, it must be noted that both these hills, and especially Caiteseal, are more easily accessed by boat across Loch Seaforth, the long, narrow sea loch lying to the west of the Pairc district. A company known as 'Wild Harris' based in the Scaladale Centre at Mairuig (GR 204062) (Tel: 07787 435621) will transport hillwalkers across the loch in a RIB and collect them again at a suitably arranged time and location. The drawback is expense – at the time of writing, this service was upwards of £200 and obviously more economical for a group of clients.

The following route description includes the walk-in to camp from Eisgein. The minor road to Eisgein begins at a junction roughly halfway between Tarbert and Stornoway, on the A859 road, easily identified by the presence of a stone memorial tower just north of the junction, on the opposite side of the road. There is a signpost to Eisgein, but it is not very prominent. Care should be taken on this road as there are very few passing places. The desolate drive to Eisgein may give the impression that this hamlet is a barren outpost of civilisation, but in fact, Eisgein is a verdant anomaly, a dear green oasis of peaceful charm and tranquillity. It occupies a natural, sheltered position at the head of a small sea loch, which itself branches off from the larger Loch Sealg.

The road abruptly ends at the entrance to Eisgein Lodge, while 30m further left is another entrance with an electrically operated metal gate (usually open). This left-hand entrance is the start of the walk. If there are no other vehicles already parked in this vicinity, then it is permissible to park hard up against the metal railing between the

Approaching Caiteseal

two entrances. (I was given permission by the kind lady who lives in the cottage just beyond the metal gate). However, if there are any problems, then return back along the road for about 400m and park at a gravelled area on the left, where there is room for several vehicles (GR 325123).

Walk through the aforementioned entrance with the electric gate, into the main estate, passing a plant nursery, several cottages and the lodge house up on the right. Turn right onto a track which climbs up to go through a kissing gate, leading south along the west side of the small sea loch, where you are likely to meet a few friendly estate ponies. In less than 1km the track turns westward through a mass of yellow gorse bushes, soon deteriorating into a sometimes-muddy footpath, following the north shore of Loch Sealg. This path is unmarked on some OS maps, but is fairly distinct and reasonably well maintained, with several new wooden footbridges and a gate through a deer fence. There is much potential wildlife to be spotted from this path, including deer, golden- and white-tailed sea eagles and red-throated divers. In clear weather, the massive bulk of Beinn Mhòr is visible directly ahead.

At the head of the sea loch lies the wreck of a small vessel, the 'Ensis', and on the opposite shore is the remains of an old township, abandoned in the mid-19th century. You may also notice a newly constructed path, snaking its way directly up the hillside, a stalker's path also used by fishermen, in order to access several hill lochs shown on the map.

Cross the tongue-twisting Abhainn Gleann Airighean Dhomhnaill by a high footbridge, before reaching a path junction 200m beyond, marked by a small cairn. Turn right here to follow an excellent, recently constructed gravel path (again unmarked on older maps) which gradually ascends westwards for over 1km to another path junction. Fork left here, gradually turning south-west to cross the Abhainn Chragoil on a fine new wooden bridge. Shortly beyond this point the path abruptly ends, but is likely to be continued at some point in the future. Just beyond the path's termination is an odd weathervane having a metal fish as the indicator.

Continue roughly south-west across boggy terrain, to reach a suitable camping area near the small lochan at GR 274092. This is less than 1km from the end of the path. In extremely dry conditions (rare!) the location of a suitable water source may be a problem, but in normal conditions there is a plethora of streams. Finding a dry spot to erect a tent is more of a challenge!

After this lengthy introduction, there now follows the route description to climb the above two hills. Begin by leaving camp and heading west to ascend the gradually steepening slopes of Sron Thorcasmol, the south-east shoulder of Beinn Mhòr. Reach a bouldery, flattish area (the shoulder) after 270m of ascent, from where the final, gently angled, stony slopes lead to the large summit cairn of Beinn Mhòr. This, the highest hill in Pairc, has, unsurprisingly, phenomenal views of the surrounding wilderness. As the crow flies, Caiteseal is still almost 4 miles away to the SSW, across awkward and uncompromising terrain.

To reach this remote summit, begin by an easy stroll along the broad south ridge to the outlying minor top of Carn Ban, whose summit on my visit was festooned by a most bizarre collection of old tyres – how and why they got there is anyone's guess. To the south and west of Carn Ban, very steep slopes

Beinn Mhòr from Caiteseal

lead down for over 300m to a deep gorge, with a stream flowing into the head of Loch Claidh, another sea loch. Leave Carn Ban in a westerly direction for some 100m of descent, before turning south and west again to descend steep grassy slopes between two craggy bluffs, bringing you down to the aforementioned stream, just south-east of the broad col at GR 238083. Caiteseal's distinctive north ridge and steep northern slopes are very obvious from here, but still a long way off, with awkward intervening ground.

Gaining the foot of Caiteseal's north ridge involves a 2km trudge across tussocky and pathless, rough terrain involving several stream crossings. As you approach Loch Chipeagil Mhòr, one of three wild lochans nestling below Caiteseal's northern slopes, the feeling of absolute remoteness is profound. The Tarbert–Stornoway road may only lie 3 miles away, but Loch Seaforth is an effective western barrier.

The lower slopes of the north ridge are fairly ill-defined, but easy-angled, with much variation possible. Higher up, a craggy steepening on the crest leads to a broad, false summit, beyond which more easy slopes lead to the small summit cairn, a lonely and

Beinn Mhòr from the Eisgein track

profoundly poignant spot to absorb the unique atmosphere of this remote location.

Time on the summit will be tempered by the realisation that it is a long way back to camp. The return route essentially retraces the outward route, but omitting a re-ascent of Beinn Mhòr. However, this still entails a further 300m of ascent, after crossing the Abhainn Gleann Claidh below Carn Ban and making a rising traverse on steep grass slopes to reach the wide bealach between Carn Ban and the wee summit of Mula na Caillich. In the upper reaches, it is easier to enter the wide gully and follow the stream up to the bealach. From here, follow the Allt Gil Bhigurra eastwards down easy slopes for 1km, before bearing north-east and contouring across the lower slopes of Sron Thorcasmol to your campsite. This completes a tiring but satisfying day.

84. GORMOL BLUE HILL (470M/1,542FT)

MAP	OS SHEET 13 OR 14 (GR 302069)
DISTANCE	22KM (FROM EISGEIN); 7KM (FROM WILDCAMP – SEE TEXT)
ASCENT	450M (FROM EISGEIN); 320M (FROM WILDCAMP)
TIME	7–9 HRS (FROM EISGEIN); 3–4 HRS (FROM WILD CAMP)
ACCESS	EISGEIN ROAD END (GR 325119 OR 325123)
DIFFICULTY	EXCELLENT TRACK AND PATHS FOR THE FIRST AND LAST 6KM – OTHERWISE FAIRLY BOGGY AND TUSSOCKY TERRAIN.
SUMMARY	Gormol is a remote summit in the heart of Lewis's Pairc district. Topographically, it has few distinguishing features, but its relative inaccessibility and unparalleled views make it a prized objective. See preceding route for map.

Summit cairn on Gormol

THE ROUTE DESCRIPTION for Gormol, outlined here, is from a wildcamp site (GR 274092), between Beinn Mhòr (see preceding route) and Gormol. The hill could be ascended on the first or third day of a 2-night/3-day camping trip. The previous route description should be read in conjunction with this one and it describes the route from the road end at Eisgein to the campsite. If you intend to climb Gormol directly from Eisgein in a day, then simply follow the route to the campsite and then take the route described here.

From camp, it is only 1km to Druim Sgianadail, the broad approach ridge to Gormol, on easy-angled grass slopes. Beyond here, make for the very obvious rocky tor, marked as a 312m spot height on the OS map. More gentle grass slopes lead from here to the summit of Gormol, in under 2km. The top is crowned by an enormous

A hazy view of the Shiants from Gormol

cairn around 4m high and is a wonderful viewpoint. Gormol's western slopes plunge steeply down for 300m to lonely lochans and wild emptiness, and the views westward and south-west eventually lead to the Shiant Isles floating on the Hebridean haze. It will be hard to leave this sublime spot.

Return to camp by the same route. If returning to Eisgein, stay on the crest of Druim Sgianadail, gradually turning north-east at its foot, to meet the approach path from the head of Loch Sealg.

85. ROINEABHAL GAELIC: POINTED HILL / NORSE: ROUGH HILL (281M/922FT)

MAP	OS SHEET 13 OR 14 (GR 233212)
DISTANCE	8KM
ASCENT	220M
TIME	3–4 HRS
ACCESS	BUS SHELTER AT BAILE AILEIN (GR 270204)
DIFFICULTY	A GOOD TRACK INITIALLY, THEN A MINOR PATH, FOLLOWED BY 'OFF GRID' TRAMPING
SUMMARY	An ideal hill for a summer evening or half day. Its summit views of the lochan studded landscape are simply breathtaking.

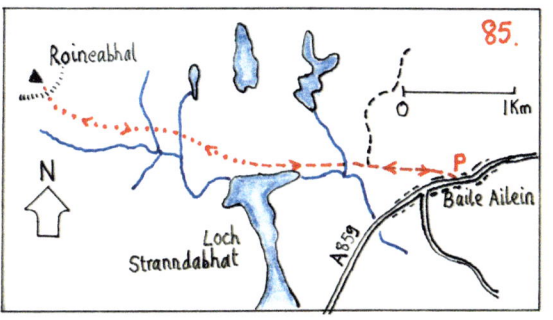

ROINEABHAL MAY NOT have the same majestic form as its namesake in South Harris, but its obvious conical bulk dominates the surrounding watery moorland. Hamish Brown, in his evocative chapter, entitled 'A day of glory given', from his excellent book *Walking the Song* (Sandstone Press), sums up the hill well when he says: 'only a modest 281 metres, it has an isolated prominence and catches the eye when seen from afar…'

The starting point for the hill's ascent is from the 'long' village of Baile Ailein, on the A859 Tarbert to Stornoway road, beginning at the bus shelter, just east of the B8060 junction. There is space behind and left of the bus shelter for a few cars, but is used much by agricultural machinery, so be careful to park considerately.

The first section of the walk follows the route of the 'Hebridean Way', a long-distance walk connecting all the main islands of the Outer Hebrides. Go through the metal gate on the right and swing left along a vehicle track heading west. Take the left fork in under 1km

The summit of Roineabhal

and go through a metal kissing gate, left of the main gate. This leads down to a small stream which is crossed on a wooden footbridge. Ignore another metal gate and instead follow the recently constructed Hebridean Way path on the left, marked by a finger post. This ash and gravel path leads shortly to Loch Stranndabhat and another metal kissing gate. Go through the gate, following the path's continuation on raised turf, for about 1km. Reach a point where the path starts to go downhill towards another wooden footbridge. This is the signal to leave the path, heading directly towards Roineabhal's mottled slopes, now only just over 1km away.

Progress from here is assisted by numerous sheep and deer trods, with the odd green, grassy knoll bearing 'the rickles of grey stones pointing to the brave people of the past' (Brown). Cross two small streams, before a gradual ascent to a wide grassy terrace, directly before the final summit cone. A girdle of small crags can be surmounted by any number of weaknesses, and beyond, it is an easy, slabby plod to the interesting summit cairn – a horseshoe drystone dyke with its back to the west, protecting the walker from prevailing westerlies.

The view northwest from Roineabhal

Nothing prepares you for the truly awe-inspiring vista north-east from the summit– the intricate and convoluted jigsaw of land and water is a microcosm of Lewis's unique landscape. Take time to sit and stare. Loch Trealabhal must be one of the most complex and contorted lochs in Scotland, its watery tentacles probing into innumerable grid squares on the map – a true wilderness. Standing in the midst of all this complexity is another wee hill – Trealabhal, at 121m. A canoe or boat would be the only practicable way of ever ascending this remote summit.

North-west of the summit is another small cairn, just a 5-minute stroll away and it is worth visiting for subtly different vistas and just to spend more time on this unique little summit.

Return by the route of ascent, to complete a short, but hugely satisfying excursion.

86. GRIOMABHAL GRIMM'S HILL (497M/1,631FT)
87. LAIBHEAL A' TUATH (505M/1,657FT)

MAP	OS SHEET 13 (GR 012220, 025244)
DISTANCE	12KM
ASCENT	850M
TIME	4.5–6 HRS
ACCESS	ROAD END, SOUTH OF MEALASTA (GR 993234)
DIFFICULTY	MOSTLY EASY, BUT PATHLESS WALKING, ON GNEISS SLABS AND SHORT GRASS
SUMMARY	A marvellous outing, traversing the beautifully slabby and craggy hills, forming the south-western quadrant of the Uig summits.

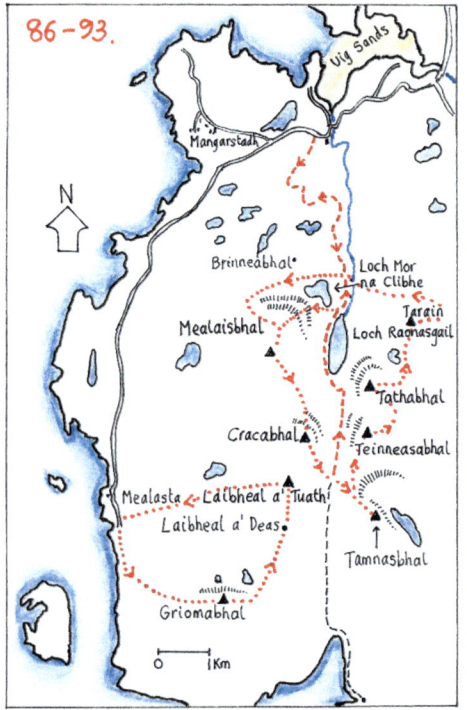

THE TRAVERSE OF these two rocky gems is Hebridean hillwalking par excellence. If rock slab 'padding' was an art form, then this route is an undoubted masterpiece, best executed in sunny conditions, when the rock is dry.

The origin of the word '*laibheal*' is obscure, but '*tuath*' means 'north' in Gaelic and the route also includes Laibheal a' Deas, ('*deas*' means 'south').

Begin at the road end, where there is a small jetty and plenty of room for parking a car. Follow the coast initially, for 1km, crossing three streams, until you are at the foot of the west ridge of Griomabhal. The ascent of this ridge is almost exclusively on superb, easy-angled gneiss

The summit of Griomabhal

En route between Griomabhal and Laibheal a' Tuath

slabs and gaining height seems almost effortless.

All too soon, reach the summit trig point, surrounded by a ring cairn. Enjoy fine views south, to remote hills and headlands, with the island of Scarp very prominent.

North of the summit, a precipitous face plunges down to lonely Dubh Loch, and further right lies the larger Loch Braighe Griomabhal, which is passed en route to the next high point. A very obvious, easy-angled, slabby spur descends from this high point, to the far side of the loch and forms the ascent route, but to reach it you will need to descend eastwards for over half a kilometre, avoiding the steep north face.

The spur provides excellent 'padding' to the tongue-twisting summit of Naideabhal a-Muigh, where again you will need to make a slight eastern detour, to avoid another steep north face. Pass a small lochan and then by a succession of rock slabs and grassy ramps, reach the summit of Laibheal a' Deas.

The final summit ridge to the highest point of the round at Laibheal a' Tuath involves very little descent or re-ascent and the route passes a scattering of wee lochans to add interest. The summit has excellent views of the other Uig hills of Cracabhal (only 1km away), and the easterly ridge of three tops, across the glen.

The view north from Laibheal a' Tuath

The long west ridge provides a fitting descent route, on short grass and slabs, passing Loch Uladail in the lower reaches. Follow the north bank of Abhainn Hotaroil down to the road and turn left to reach the jetty in only a few hundred metres.

88. MEALAISBHAL FARMSTEAD HILL OR HONEY HILL (574M/1,883FT)
89. CRACABHAL CROW HILL OR CREVICED HILL (514M/1,686FT)

MAP	OS SHEET 13 (GR 022270, 030253)
DISTANCE	17KM OR 19KM
ASCENT	740M
TIME	6–8 HRS
ACCESS	START OF RAONASGAIL TRACK (GR 032314)
DIFFICULTY	GOOD APPROACH AND RETURN TRACK; VERY ROUGH, PATHLESS WALKING, WITH OPTIONAL SCRAMBLING ON THE HILL
SUMMARY	A wild and rocky walk and climb to the highest hill in Lewis, together with its craggy southern neighbour. See preceding route for map.

THE COMPACT GROUP of hills, south of the Uig Sands, are undoubtedly the finest in Lewis; displaying a wild mountainous character and isolation, which ensures they receive relatively few visitors. Their general topography is fairly straightforward: two lines of hills on a north–south axis, separated by the straight glens of Raonasgail and Tamanisdale.

The ascent of all eight main summits in a single day is for hardened hill-goers only, and this guide conveniently splits them into three separate and manage-able expeditions. The following route description is an ideal introduction to this intriguing, remote area.

Start walking up the Glen Raonasgail track, from the minor coast road near Uig Sands, and follow this for about

Approach track to the Uig hills

3km to the vicinity of Loch Mòr na Clibhe, nestling directly beneath the impressive, north facing crags and cliffs of Mula Mac Sgiathain, forming the vertiginous, northern shoulder of your first objective, Mealaisbhal.

At this point, a decision will have to be made. Confident scramblers could continue along the track and climb the obvious, slabby buttress, rising directly

Tathabhal from Mealaisbhal

up from the southern, indented side of the loch. With good route-finding skills, this is an excellent ascent route and any intimidating situations can be circumvented – I talk from experience! Easier options are generally left of the buttress. If the rock is at all wet, then leave well enough alone and consider the following alternative.

For those who are already put off just reading the previous paragraph, or who are not scramblers, the easiest, but dogleg option, is to head west, staying north of the loch, between the wee hill of Brinneabhal and the cliffs on your left. After 2km, turn south, then southeast, up steep but grassy slopes to reach the north shoulder of Mealaisbhal.

Both of the aforementioned routes arrive on the crest of the north shoulder, from where an easy 100m of ascent, on stony terrain, leads to the summit of Mealaisbhal, a terrific viewpoint, particularly north and westward. On a clear day, you may spot the Flannan Isles and St Kilda.

The northern spur of Mealaisbhal from Loch Mor na Clibhe

Tamnasbhal from Cracabhal

The summit area and south flank of Mealaisbhal is a complex mass of huge boulders and slabs, so during the descent, south-east to the col below Cracabhal, keep further left to avoid the worst. At the col, pass three tiny lochans, before beginning the steep, rocky ascent to Cracabhal. The climb involves a maze of large blocks and terraces, but is perfectly straightforward. From the summit, enjoy a fine view south, down the glen and the recently constructed track to the head of the remote sea loch, Cheann Chuisil, with the higher Harris hills beyond.

An easy descent, south-east, drops 250m to the high point on the track, where you turn left for the long, but relaxing, 7km return saunter to the road.

90. TAMNASBHAL POSSIBLY HILL OF REFUGE (467M/1,532FT)
91. TEINNEASABHAL SEE TEXT (497M/1,631FT)
92. TATHABHAL JOINING HILL (515M/,1690FT)
93. TARAIN ORIGIN OBSCURE (411M/1,348FT)

MAP	OS SHEET 13 (GR 043237, 041254, 042264, 051277)
DISTANCE	21KM
ASCENT	950M
TIME	7–9 HRS
ACCESS	START OF GLEN RAONASGAIL TRACK (GR 032314)
DIFFICULTY	AN EXCELLENT TRACK AT THE BEGINNING AND END, BUT THE MAIN HILL TRAVERSE IS PATHLESS, RUGGED AND ROCKY, IN-VOLVING SOME TRICKY DESCENTS IN COMPLEX TERRAIN; GOOD ROUTE-FINDING IS ESSENTIAL FOR THIS DEMANDING OUTING; FOR EXPERIENCED HILL WALKERS ONLY
SUMMARY	The traverse of the four 'Tees' is one of the best hill tramps in Lewis, with stunning views of remote, wild country and distant beaches. Save this one for a clear day! See Routes 86, 87 for map.

THE ORIGIN OF the names of these four hills is a mixture of Gaelic and Norse. The word '*teinne*' in Gaelic can mean both tightness or a link of a chain and the latter could refer to the four hills forming a chain of summits on the east side of Glen Raonasgail.

As hinted in the previous route description, parking is very limited at the end of the Glen Raonasgail track and you should not block access to the road. Walk up the track, with an eye out for red deer and possibly golden eagles, as well as white-tailed eagles, all very prominent in this vicinity. It will take the best part of 2 hours to reach the high point of the track, passing Loch Raonasgail and the soaring granite and Lewisian gneiss buttresses, forming the west faces of Tathabhal and Teinneasabhal.

At the high point, leave the track on the left and ascend easy grass slopes, gaining 100m in height, to reach the wide bealach between Tamnasbhal and Teinneasabhal. Amble up the gentle northwest ridge of Tamnasbhal, to reach its flat summit area in under 1km. Unfortunately, the wild Loch Dhiobadail, east of the peak, is not visible from the summit, but the view south and west, of remote hills and sea lochs more than compensates. The actual summit is little more than a

The view north from Teinneasabhal of Mealaisbhal and Loch Raonasgail

boulder perched on a flat slab.

Retrace steps to the bealach and climb easy-angled grass slopes, interspersed with occasional rock slabs and small crags, to reach the substantial cairn forming the summit of Teinneasabhal. Just before the summit, there is a dramatic view looking down and along Glen Raonasgail, with the track far below, winding its way along the glen, and the white sands of Uig in the far distance.

The next peak, Tathabhal, lies directly north of here, but rather than descending north, head north-east from the summit, in order to avoid steep crags. This descent, however, is just a warm-up for the descent of the next two hills, which involve much more complex and convoluted terrain. Reach the wide bealach below Tathabhal, with its two tiny lochans, and climb the slightly steeper grass slopes of Tathabhal, trending right to avoid crags. The summit, at 515m, is the highest of the walk and is crowned by another cairn. Enjoy another superb view looking north, past Loch Raonasgail to sand and sea.

Tathabhal has very steep cliffs and crags on its north side and it is imperative to initially descend almost directly eastward from the summit, to be sure of finding the easiest line.

A series of heathery gullies and ramps lead gradually downwards, eventually arriving at the picturesque Loch Mòr Bràigh Tarain, the larger of two lochans at the col. Bypass this lochan on its eastern side and begin the easy ascent of the last peak of the day, Tarain. Tarain is an altogether rockier ascent than the previous hills, but nowhere difficult and offering a profusion of beautiful easy-angled slabs for a rapid ascent. The final summit cone is a grand slabby short climb, with numerous scrambling lines and is crowned by a small cairn.

Despite Tarain being the lowest summit of the four, its topography is highly complex and rugged, hosting a profusion of craggy cul-de-sacs to trap the unwary and its descent will require much care

The view north from Tarain

The final rocky summit cone of Tarain

and attention. As with Tathabhal, the wisest option is to head east initially, scouting the route ahead for the easiest line between steep crags. Gradually, head more north as you descend, keeping in mind that you are making for the small lochan below Cleite Adhamh (GR 050282). It is easy to lose too much height and you may need to reascend to gain the security of the col, with its lochan. A compass may be useful, even in clear weather, to reach this point.

From the lochan, head west, following the line of its outflow stream, on easy-angled grass slopes, before crossing the outflow stream of Loch Raonasgail, to reach the approach track. Turn right, and walk the final 4km to the start.

For those whose appetite for craggy peaks has been whetted, it is worth noting that north of Tarain, there are several other very rocky and prominent smaller summits, such as Beannan a' Deas (GR 055292) which are worth exploring. These are best approached from the road end at the north of Loch Suaineabhal (the starting point for Suaineabhal and Sron ri Gaoith).

94. SUAINEABHAL WINDING HILL (429M/1,407FT)
95. SRON RI GAOITH NOSE TO THE WIND (253M/830FT)

MAP	OS SHEET 13 (GR 078309, 075292)
DISTANCE	7KM
ASCENT	590M
TIME	4–5 HRS
ACCESS	ROAD END, NORTH LOCH SUAINEABHAL (GR 064310)
DIFFICULTY	A SHORT, BUT MAINLY PATHLESS WALK OVER RELATIVELY CHALLENGING TERRAIN, WITH AN EXPOSED LOCH SIDE TRAIL ON THE RETURN LEG
SUMMARY	This relatively short ramble over two rugged and exposed Lewis hills offers a rewarding half day's outing and is a good introduction to Lewis's wild landscape.

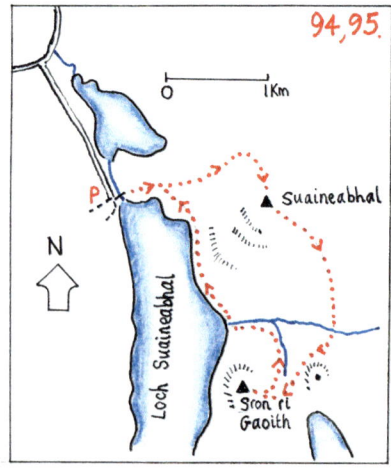

THE STARTING POINT for the walk lies a short distance from the famed Uig Sands, at the end of the short road leading to Loch Suaineabhal, where there is a good parking area on the right. A signpost indicating a cross-country walk to Carishader is initially followed over the weir at the end of the loch, on a metal bridge.

Ahead, the imposing bulk of Suaineabhal dominates the view, while further to the right, across the loch, Sron ri Gaoith is very prominent. Follow a line of posts on a boggy path for about half a kilometre, before branching off to the right to ascend an obvious wide terrace of heather, grass and boulders, gradually moving up leftwards below steeper ground. Once more level terrain is reached, ascend rightward into a heather-choked depression between crags, on a vague path. The angle soon eases to a series of hummocks and crags, with the large, well-constructed summit cairn perched precariously on an exposed

Sron ri Gaoith from Loch Suaineabhal

crag. Enjoy superb panoramic views, especially north-west to the Uig Sands and the blue expanse beyond.

From the summit, take a south-easterly line downwards, to reach a broad

Suaineabhal from Sron ri Gaoith

grassy ramp leading to the wide bealach east of Sron ri Gaoith. Continue round the north side of the small hill of Oirchlest, descending slightly, before ascending Sron ri Gaoith by its lower grass slopes, followed by a steeper heather section between crags. The summit cairn is small and offers a fine retrospective view of Suaineabhal, with its namesake loch to the left.

Descend the same way and follow a stream which flows into the loch on the north side of the peak. Pick up a sheep/deer track on the opposite side of the stream, which follows a line of about 15m above the loch, along steep

The summit of Suaineabhal

ground, forming the lower slopes of Suaineabhal. This path begins fairly benignly, but there is one quite exposed section around a craggy bluff which will concentrate the mind. Care here is certainly required! Finally, reach the flat, tussocky ground at the head of the loch, leading back to the start.

96. BEINN BHRAGAIR TANGLED TOPS HILL? (261M/856FT)

MAP	OS SHEET 8 (GR 267433)
DISTANCE	7KM
ASCENT	220M
TIME	2–3 HRS
ACCESS	PAIRC SHIABOIST ROAD END (GR 267457)
DIFFICULTY	GOOD APPROACH AND RETURN TRACKS, WITH PATHLESS, HEATH-ERY HILLWALKING
SUMMARY	A short ascent of the finest hill in North Lewis.

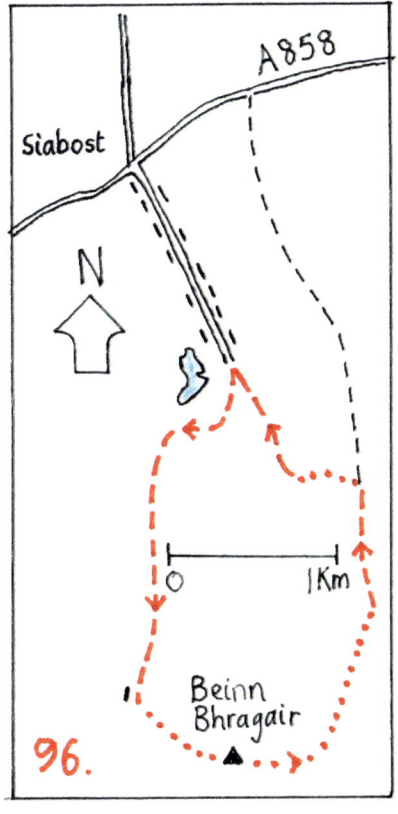

OUT OF THE handful of small hills rising from the blanket peat bog of North Lewis, Beinn Bhragair may not be the highest, but is certainly the one with attitude and character. Its craggy appearance and ease of access from the north make it a fairly popular wee hill with locals and visitors alike.

From the A858 take the Pairc Shiaboist road and park near the end of the road at a suitable spot. The road end is a turning circle for buses, so ensure your car is free of this area. Go through the gate and walk along the eroded tarmac road, round a large bend, gradually ascending, with Beinn Bhragair directly ahead. Reach an old water treatment building at the end of the road and turn off to the left to begin the ascent. There is no obvious path, but the numerous crags are easily breached by heather ledges and gullies. Towards the top, the angle eases and you will soon reach the cairn and trig point standing on a rocky wart.

The view from Beinn Bhragair

The summit view is a vast panorama of peat moorland, lochans and the odd cottage, with other small hills breaking the horizon. Beyond is the flat blue of the Atlantic.

To vary the descent, head eastward from the summit and cross a grassy gully to reach a spur, which heads down northwards to reach the end of another track crossing the moor. Follow this for 1km, before breaking off to the left, to join a third less distinct grassy track leading directly back to the gate and your departure point.

GETTING TO LEWIS

CalMac offer services including Uig to Tarbert (Harris) and Ullapool to Stornoway (Lewis). See CalMac website for details. Flights are also available to Stornoway from various Scottish airports. See Loganair website for details.

ST KILDA (Hirta)

97. OISEBHAL EAST FELL – OLD ICELANDIC (293M/961FT)
98. CONACHAIR SEE TEXT (430M/1,411FT)
99. MULLACH BI PILLAR SUMMIT (358M/1,174FT)

MAP	OS SHEET 18 (GR 109992, 100003, 080994)
DISTANCE	10KM
ASCENT	640M
TIME	3–5 HRS
ACCESS	VILLAGE BAY (SEE END FOR ST KILDA ACCESS)
DIFFICULTY	GRASSY HILLWALKING AND TRACKS, WITH POTENTIALLY HAZARDOUS CLIFF EDGE WALKING
SUMMARY	This circuit of the main summits above Village Bay, including St Kilda's highest point, is for many walkers, a once-in-a-lifetime experience.

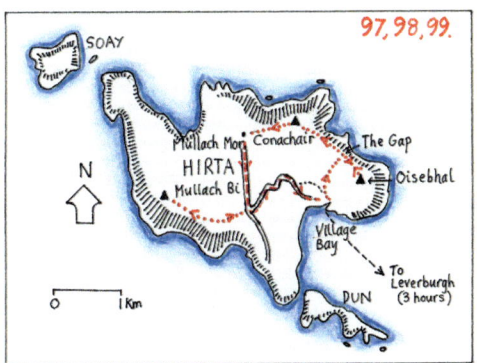

HIRTA IS THE largest of the St Kilda archipelago, comprising Britain's most remote islands, lying some 40 miles west of the Outer Hebrides. The rocky islands and stacks are all that remain of a 60-million-year-old vast volcano, the rim of which defines the south and west coasts of Hirta and Soay.

The name St Kilda does not refer to a saint, but likely evolved as a translational error from the Old Icelandic '*skildar*', meaning 'shields', describing the shape of the islands when seen from afar.

Despite its remoteness and inaccessibility, Hirta supported a population of hardy souls, until their evacuation in 1930, with a flurry of publicity. St Kilda's public profile has risen considerably since then, and the archipelago has been designated a double UNESCO World Heritage Site, due to its historical

Boreray from Hirta

Boreray and the Stacks from
Connachair's summit

and cultural significance, as well as its unique environmental and scenic value. For most, St Kilda is a 'bucket list' destination and a once-in-a-lifetime trip.

As time on Hirta is at a premium, it is advisable to complete the walk first, allowing time to explore Village Bay before departure. Begin by heading north-east from the bay up into the grassy depression known as An Lag (the hollow in the north). This ice-hollowed bowl contains ancient stone circles in the rough shape of a boat, dating back to 1850 BC and are the earliest known monuments on St Kilda. Of more recent construction are the numerous stone structures known as cleits, used by St Kildans to store turf (peat), which then dried and could be used for fuel.

In under half an hour you will reach 'the Gap', the wild and windy defile between Oisebhal and Conachair and a truly awe-inspiring spot to view Boreray and the Stacks, some 4 miles to the north-east. There is also a marvellous view of Village Bay and the jagged knife-edge of Dun, a natural breakwater for the bay.

The summit of Oisebhal lies less than 1km south of here and is easily reached by turning right and following the cliff edge up gentle grass slopes, with dizzying views down to the churning sea below. After a height gain of about 120m, reach the flattish summit of Oisebhal, where there is a cracking bird's-eye view of the arc of cottages in Village Bay. The eastern extremity of Oisebhal ends in Rubha an Uisge, (headland of the waters) where the thin veil of a waterfall tumbles down the granite cliffs to the sea.

Retrace steps to the Gap and continue upwards, following the cliff edge north-west for about 200m. Here, you can gaze down the precipice to a massive grassy hollow, tucked in under the cliffs below Conachair. It is a great place to view fulmars, puffins, shags and Manx shearwaters, and you may spot seals hauled up on the rocks far below. The St Kildans even kept sheep here, over the winter.

As you continue upwards, the threat of great skuas (bonxies) is highly likely – a trekking pole held above the head is a good foil for these enormous birds' dive-bombing antics. The true summit of Conachair lies a few hundred metres north of the stone trig point and is marked by a small cairn.

The name 'Conachair' has a multitude of possible meanings, ranging from 'beacon', 'landmark' and 'uproar' to lengthier interpretations, such as 'the coming together of the hills' and even 'a sick person who neither gets better nor worse'! The most likely meaning is the 'place of the folds' according to Peter Drummond's thoroughly researched book, *Scottish Hill Names*.

The Conachair cliffs to the north are the highest sea cliffs in Britain, although less continuously vertical than the Kame on Foula, in Shetland (see Route 53), or St John's Head on Hoy (see Routes 51, 52). They are home to some thousand pairs of fulmars. On a clear day, the views from Conachair are quite stunning and you may well spot the Cuillin ridge of Skye,

100 miles distant.

Leave Conachair by its grassy west ridge and head to the spacious summit of Mullach Mòr (the big hill summit), conspicuous due to the massive radar station perched on its crest, somewhat out of character in this wild spot. Also out of character is the tarmac road, running south along the ridge, separating Village Bay and Gleann Mor, the vast, wild and rocky corrie to the west.

The final summit of Mullach Bi lies in a south-westerly direction, across the bowl of Gleann Mor and is the high point of Hirta's westerly seaward ridge. To reach it, follow the road south for 1km, to the head of the glen. Just before the junction with the road descending to Village Bay, turn off to a right, on a track which gradually disappears. Beyond here, an old earth dyke, built by the locals in order to keep their cattle in Gleann Mor, can be followed, before

Approaching Mullach Bi

Soay from Mullach Bi

reaching the high, rocky headland known as Claigeann Mor (skull rock). From here, there is a magnificent view of Mullach Bi, the crowning glory of Hirta's west cliffs.

En route to the summit, you will pass the famous Lover's Stone, consisting of a huge, overhanging slab and often confused with the Mistress Stone on Ruabhal. Continue along the cliff edge on short grass to eventually reach Mullach Bi, the second highest point on Hirta. This is easily the most dramatic summit on the island, its western slopes dropping precipitously to the sea and offering tremendous views in all directions. There is also a first view of Soay, another island lying north-west of Hirta.

Retrace steps to the tarmac road and turn right then left to descend to Village Bay. Be sure to spend time exploring the picturesque arc of stone cottages and absorb the atmosphere and history of this incredible place.

GETTING TO ST KILDA

Due to its unique and popular status, many boat tour operators offer trips to St Kilda and certainly too many to list here. Not all sail from Harris/Lewis either; some offer trips from Skye and even from Oban. Check online for all options, prices and availability.

BORERAY

100. MULLACH AN EILEIN SUMMIT OF THE ISLAND (384M/1,259FT)

MAP	OS SHEET 18 (GR 155054)
DISTANCE	2.5KM
ASCENT	384M
TIME	1–2 HRS
ACCESS	SOUTH-WEST LANDING SITE (GR 154045); FOR BORERAY ACCESS, SEE TEXT
DIFFICULTY	POTENTIAL DIFFICULTIES OF BOTH ISLAND ACCESS AND TERRAIN; A SERIOUS UNDERTAKING
SUMMARY	In favourable conditions, a Boreray landing and subsequent climb to its highest point is truly the stuff of dreams and certainly for me, it is still a bucket-list wish.

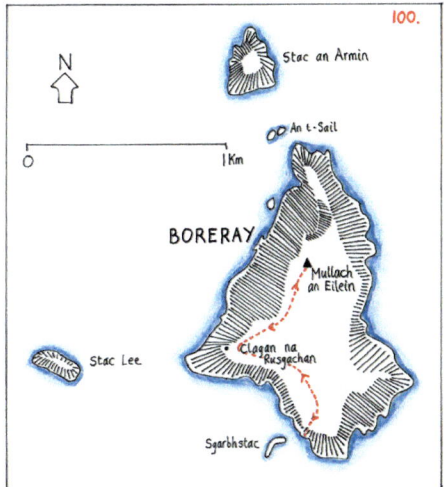

BORERAY (THE FORTIFIED isle) and its sea-stack neighbours, Stac Lee and Stac an Armin, lie some 4 miles from the main island of Hirta, and in suitable conditions, are usually visited by boat, following a Hirta landing, by the main St Kilda boat operators. These visits, however, are strictly non-landing and with good reason. Boreray's coastline is a continuous bastion of spectacular, vertiginous cliffs, steep and slippery slabs and raging chasms. Of the precious few chinks in this impressive armour that do exist, an extended mooring is simply impossible, and tenders are required to gain access to rock slabs, provided that the swell is within a manageable limit.

In extremely calm conditions, the above landing site is the most favourable

Boreray's craggy sea defences

but later, as on Hirta, turf or peat was kept in them for fires. This is a fantastic vantage point, looking out to Stac Lee, resembling a gigantic shark's fin or tooth.

Head north on a gradually rising path, passing the remains of three bothies on the left. These were sturdy affairs, built into the hillside, with only one still having the protective earth wall standing. The hardiest St Kildans would come over from Hirta, complete with burning peat in a pot, straw bedding, kindling sticks, fowling rods and a creel basket containing meat, oatcakes, scones and the like, to last a week or two.

In 1759 however, 10 men spent longer than they bargained for, when a storm blew up and they were stranded on Boreray from October until the following June, surviving on birds and sheep. They were eventually rescued by the steward 'without sustaining any great loss, other being much out of humour' – an understatement by any means!

Ahead and left of the summit, there is an immense three-pronged rock tower, known as Clagan na Rusgachan, (skull rock of the fleeces) standing 240m above the sea. Below the summit is a natural defile, where the St Kildans sheared their sheep – hence the name. The highest concentration of nesting

and was regularly used by the St Kildans, who came across to harvest gannets and to shear the sheep. Other sites are possible and have indeed been used by recent parties, but are not recommended, as bird disturbance is a problem and can be dangerous, due to slippery rock and steep terrain. Note also, that before any landing is attempted, permission will be required from the NTS warden on Hirta. A landing on Boreray will require a perfect storm of patience, determination, organisation and luck.

Assuming that everything has come together and you have made your first footfall on Boreray... walk carefully up the steep slabs, avoiding wet or greasy rock. Some parties have resorted to using micro spikes on the soles of their boots on some of the steeper landing sites. On reaching grass, the angle begins to lessen and you will eventually arrive at a group of cleits, some 130m above the sea. Originally, these were used to store gannets,

gannets is found here (some 2,000 pairs), and the ledges used by the St Kildans to hunt the gannets are very well defined.

The spectacular cliffs of Boreray

An arête and cliff edge lead naturally upwards from the rock tower, and this is followed until you are gazing down into a huge, cavernous hollow, known as Clais na Runaich (furrow of the beloved), where grassy areas support a large puffin colony. Stac Lee is now far below, with the Hirta group beyond.

Continue up the cliff edge, until you reach the final, steep grass slope, leading to the summit on the right. Make a rising traverse left here, to arrive on the slightly lower west summit, known as Na Roachan, (wrinkled rocks?). This is an awesome rock tower of 382m, with gargantuan buttresses and cliffs, dropping sheer to the pounding waves far below – an absolutely awe-inspiring spot (I imagine!)

From here, walk east, descending slightly, before ascending the final grassy slope, over a series of curious undulations, with spectacular drops on the left. Reach Boreray's highest point and look north down the dizzying depths of a vertiginous gully, rising from Geo na Tarnanach (thunder cave), forming a natural barrier to any further exploration by walkers. Beyond is the massive, split tower of An t-Sail (the heel), and Stac an Armin beyond.

The sense of urgency to return to your only means of return to civilisation, may just curtail the notion of any extended stay on this unique summit. Return by the outward route, taking extra care on the steep grass slopes.

As a final word of warning: it may be necessary, but certainly advisable, to stay in contact with the boatman during your ascent, as quickly changing sea conditions may necessitate a change of departure point.

GETTING TO BORERAY

Boreray is the most difficult to access of all the islands in this book. There is no regular access and permission to land will be required from the NTS. Contact NTS website for details.

Index of Hill Names and Islands

(Islands are listed with capital letters)
(Hills marked * are not Marilyns)

AILSA CRAIG 22
An Cruachan 90
An Sgùrr 73
ARRAN 28
BARRA 143
Beinn a' Bhraghad 90
Beinn a' Ghraig 57
Beinn Bheigier 33
Beinn Bhragair 213
Beinn Ceann a' Mhara * 70
Beinn Choradail 152
Beinn Chreagach 68
Beinn Dhubh 171
Beinn Mhòr 191
Beinn na Cro 80
Beinn na Duatharach 59
Beinn na h-Iolaire 124
Beinn na Sreine 54
Beinn Ruigh Choinnich 149
Beinn Sciathan 147
Beinn Tangabhal 145
BENBECULA 155
Ben Dearg 107
Ben Tianavaig 96
Bioda Buidhe 111
Biod an Athair 103
Bleabhal 167
Bloodstone Hill * 76
BORERAY 219

The Cairn 22
Caiteseal 191
Carnan 140
Carnan Eoin * 46
Ceapabhal 169
Ceartabhal * 178
Cleat * 111
COLONSAY 46
Conachair 215
Corra Bheinn 43
Cracabhal 204
Creach Bheinn 54
Cruach Scarba 49
Cuilags 130
DAVAAR 31
Davaar summit * 31
Da Sneug 133
Dùn Caan (Cana) 121
Dun I * 66
Dun Mor * 117
Eabhal 157
EIGG 73
ERISKAY 147
Feiriosbhal 188
FOULA 133
GARBH EILEAN (SHIANTS) 184
Giolabhal Glas * 202
Glas Bheinn (Islay) 33
Glas Bheinn (Jura) 41
Glas Bheinn Mhòr 80
Gormol 197
Griomabhal 202

223

Guaineamol	188
HARRIS	165
Heabhal (Barra)	143
Healabhal Bheag (Skye)	98
Healabhal Mhòr (Skye)	98
HIRTA	215
HOLY ISLAND	25
HOY	130
Huiseabhal Mòr	178
IONA	66
ISLAY	33
JURA	41
Laibheal a' Tuath *	202
Leac nan Fionn *	117
Leosabhal *	178
LEWIS	188
Lì a Tuath	160
Liuthaid *	181
Mealaisbhal	204
Meall nan Damh	28
Meall na Suiramach	114
MINGULAY	140
Muaitheabhal	188
MULL	54
Mullach an Eilein	219
Mullach Bi *	215
Mullach Buidhe	184
Mullach Mòr	25
NORTH UIST	157
Oisebhal *	215
Orval	76
Preshal Beg *	93
Preshal More *	93
Quiraing East Peak *	114
RAASAY	121
Roineabhal (Harris)	199
Roineabhal (Lewis)	199
Ruabhal *	155
Ruadh Stac	88
RUM	76
'S Àirde Beinn	64
SCARBA	49
Scrinadle	43
Sgaoth Aird	173
Sgarbh Breac	39
Sgòrr nam Faoileann	36
Sgùrr a Mhadaidh Ruaidh *	109
Sgùrr na Strì	83
SHIANT ISLANDS	184
Sithean Bhealaich Chumhaing	105
SKYE	80
SOUTH UIST	149
Speinne Mòr	62
Sron ri Gaoith *	210
Sron Vourlinn *	114
Stulabhal (South Uist)	149
Stulabhal (Harris)	181
Suaineabhal	210
Tamnasbhal *	207
Tarain *	207
Tathabhal	207
Teinneasabhal *	207
Thacla (Hecla)	152
TIREE	70
Todun	176
Triuirebheinn	149
ULVA	68
Ward Hill	130
Waterstein Head *	101

Luath Press Limited

committed to publishing well written books worth reading

LUATH PRESS takes its name from Robert Burns, whose little collie Luath (*Gael.*, swift or nimble) tripped up Jean Armour at a wedding and gave him the chance to speak to the woman who was to be his wife and the abiding love of his life. Burns called one of the 'Twa Dogs' Luath after Cuchullin's hunting dog in Ossian's *Fingal*. Luath Press was established in 1981 in the heart of Burns country, and is now based a few steps up the road from Burns' first lodgings on Edinburgh's Royal Mile. Luath offers you distinctive writing with a hint of unexpected pleasures.

Most bookshops in the UK, the US, Canada, Australia, New Zealand and parts of Europe, either carry our books in stock or can order them for you. To order direct from us, please send a £sterling cheque, postal order, international money order or your credit card details (number, address of cardholder and expiry date) to us at the address below. Please add post and packing as follows: UK – £1.00 per delivery address; overseas surface mail – £2.50 per delivery address; overseas airmail – £3.50 for the first book to each delivery address, plus £1.00 for each additional book by airmail to the same address. If your order is a gift, we will happily enclose your card or message at no extra charge.

Luath Press Limited
543/2 Castlehill
The Royal Mile
Edinburgh EH1 2ND
Scotland
Telephone: 0131 225 4326 (24 hours)
Email: sales@luath.co.uk
Website: www.luath.co.uk